A Political Analysis
of Student Activism:
The Turkish Case

JOSEPH S. SZYLIOWICZ

University of Denver

SAGE PUBLICATIONS / Beverly Hills / London

Copyright © 1972 by Sage Publications, Inc.

Printed in the United States of America

All rights reserved. No part of this book may be reproduced
or utilized in any form or by any means, electronic or mechanical,
including photocopying, recording, or by any
information storage and retrieval system, without permission in writing
from the publisher.

For information address:

SAGE PUBLICATIONS, INC.
275 South Beverly Drive
Beverly Hills, California 90212

SAGE PUBLICATIONS LTD
St George's House / 44 Hatton Garden
London E C 1

International Standard Book Number 0-8039-0188-7

Library of Congress Catalog Card No. 72-89163

FIRST PRINTING

CONTENTS

Introduction 5

The Ottoman Empire 15

The Young Turks and World War I 21

The One-Party Era (1923-1946) 24

The Multiparty Era (1946-1960) 34

From Revolution to Intervention 51

Conclusion 66

Notes 71

References 72

Appendix 77

A Political Analysis
of Student Activism:
The Turkish Case

JOSEPH S. SZYLIOWICZ
University of Denver

INTRODUCTION

In recent years, student activism has become a commonplace phenomenon in almost every country of the world, even the United States, whose campuses had, in the fifties, been widely characterized as the home of an apathetic generation. One result of the outbreak of violence at Berkeley, Columbia, Kent State, and elsewhere has been to spur a flood of studies that have attempted to analyze the character of the American student movement and its leaders and participants. When these books are added to the continually proliferating literature on students in other societies, it would appear that the topic of student activism suffers from severe overexposure and that little remains to be written on this subject.[1]

Even a cursory examination of the literature, however, reveals that this is not really the case. Despite the fact that students of practically no

AUTHOR'S NOTE: *I must express my thanks to the many Turkish student leaders of various periods who made this study possible and the field research a most exciting and rewarding experience. The study was conducted under a fellowship from the American Research Institute in Turkey and the GSIS/SSF provided financial and secretarial support during the writing stage. My ideas have been profoundly influenced by ongoing discussions with colleagues and students at GSIS. I am especially grateful to John McCamant and Mrs. Mary Jane Hogan for their comments and suggestions. Mr. Harvey Silverstein contributed greatly to the elaboration of the present conceptual framework. Harry Eckstein and Ted Gurr also provided valuable criticisms.*

country have escaped the attention of American scholars, the coverage of available studies is very uneven. Some countries, particularly those in Latin America and India, have been the subject of numerous books and articles, whereas others, like Turkey, where students have played an important role for many years in its political life, have been largely neglected.[2] One of the purposes of this monograph is to remedy this situation for Turkey.

More important than uneven geographical coverage, however, are the serious intellectual shortcomings that characterize the available literature. Generally speaking, there has been a notable absence of sophisticated theorizing as well as of systematic empirical research, so that it should not be particularly surprising to learn that results have been noncomparable and contradictory or that the field remains dominated by "speculation and opinions" (Scott and El-Assal, 1969: 702; also Tygart and Holt, 1972: 957-958). Moreover, although student activism is essentially a political phenomenon, none of the commonly used approaches emphasize political variables (Weinberg and Walker, 1969: 79-81; Pinner, 1971: 128).

Essentially, three perspectives can be identified, and most scholars have adopted one or a combination of these. The first consists of a focus upon individual actors as scholars have attempted, by looking at data concerning such variables as age, socioeconomic background, and personality characteristics to identify the common attributes of activists and to differentiate them from other students. Horn and Knott (1971) have analyzed the findings of numerous studies of this sort and their conclusions may be summarized as follows:

(1) Activists were a minority both of the students and of their peer groups;

(2) could be clearly differentiated from "hippies" who had "dropped out" and who were estranged from their parents, whereas activists possessed similar values and patterns of beliefs as did their parents;

(3) tended to be of liberal, upper-class backgrounds;

(4) were of sound mental health and were guided by high ethical and moral principles; and

(5) were better students and more intellectually oriented than other students.

Other social scientists have viewed student unrest as a group phenomenon of social protest, and they have utilized a different approach, often examining institutional factors to analyze historical and contemporary developments. When looking at the university environment, they have discussed such variables as the quality of the institution, its location, size, facilities, the administrative structure, the relations between students and faculty, the degree of bureaucratization, and the like. Thus, one scholar has concluded after discussing various aspects of the university environment in different societies: "Far more important than the university's location and auspices in accounting for student inquietudes [unrest] and indiscipline is the quality of university life." He explains the difference in levels of activism between African institutions and those in Latin America and Asia by arguing that the former are marked by elitist systems whose graduates are confident of future employment, and he continues:

> in the university where underpaid, part-time professors lecture to anonymous crowds, where 'education' means passing examinations and 'learning' means cramming for them, where the student is unsupervised, unstimulated and, finally, unrewarded—under these conditions, student unrest is almost inevitable [Emmerson, 1968: 401].

Though statements of this kind abound in the literature, at least two reservations must be entered. First, it is necessary, for analytical purposes, to separate the actual opportunities open to graduates or the students' perceptions thereof, from academic weaknesses. We shall return to this point later. Second, it is not clear whether the quality of education is, in fact, an important variable. Studies in the United States have demonstrated that, as we have noted, activists tended to be better students than other students and were therefore likely to have established closer ties with faculty, participated in special programs, and the like. Other studies have shown that protesters rated their education as highly as did other students. Furthermore, one detailed study uncovered no relationship whatsoever between institutional characteristics and the number of student protesters on campus. When differences in the freshman class were controlled for, only 1 of 58 features of the institution—the presence of an active fine arts program— was found to be significant. None of the others, including degree of student involvement, cohesiveness of the campus, administration student policies, the formality of classes, and the like, were found to be related to the degree of student involvement in activism (Kenniston and Lerner, 1970). In short, the relationship between the character of the university environment and student activism is an ambiguous one. Nevertheless, it will represent part of the student subsystem within our conceptualization and, in our discussion, we shall include enough data on this topic to provide an appropriate perspective for our analysis of the Turkish case.

The third common focus has been upon such societal aspects as generational conflict, the impact of advanced technology and rapid growth, the history of social protest within a state, the impact of predominant norms and values, and so forth. Thus Kenniston (1965) argues that activism is a form of generational conflict which is aggravated in advanced societies because adolescence is prolonged, and Klineberg (1971) suggests that in modernizing states students confront an identity crisis unknown in traditional societies. Similarly, Lipset (1970) attributes outbursts of protest in the United States to the liberal development of American society.

Many of these studies provide valuable insights into various aspects of student activism, but cumulation and replication remain elusive, and few theoretical or empirical advances are yet apparent, particularly in comparative analysis. Part of the problem stems from the fact that far too often theoretical contexts have been weak, and research designs have been operationalized in a noncomparable manner and implemented in a rather haphazard fashion. The result has been confusion and fundamental disagreement as to the relevance and impact of specific variables, and it is no great exaggeration to suggest that, as we have demonstrated in the case of institutional factors, one simply cannot draw any firm conclusions concerning the impact or relevance of particular variables in different settings. The existing state of the field can be vividly illustrated by the following summary of the relationship between social background and politicization:

> Several studies have shown that upwardly mobile students tend to be more politicized than those from higher-status backgrounds. Evidence also exists for several countries suggesting that lower-status backgrounds are conducive to radical leftist views. But other investigations indicate the opposite: that upwardly mobile students are likely to be *less* politicized and *less* radical. Finally, there is also evidence for the hypothesis that social status is not related, or at least not unambiguously related, to politicization or radicalism [Emmerson, 1968: 395].

Clearly the level of generalization that is possible under these circumstances is quite limited, and the continuing proliferation of contradictory data further hampers development of the field.

The second major weakness of most studies is the practically blatant disregard of political variables. Even when political scientists have analyzed student activism, they have tended to neglect or ignore the political dimension, and to utilize one of the approaches discussed earlier. Thus, though it may well be banal to point out that the character of the political system fundamentally shapes the scope, character, and intensity of student activism, only recently—and even now quite rarely—have scholars begun to recognize the limitations of nonpolitical approaches and to note the need to relate such studies to the particular political system in which activism occurs.

This point has recently been emphasized by Lipset (1970: 497), one of the most perceptive analysts of student activism both in the United States and abroad, who has rightly pointed out:

> Essentially, the sources of political activism *among* students must be found in politics, in the factors associated with different types of politics. The explanations for more political activism at one time rather than another must also be found on a political level, in the sources of variations in political response.

Subsequently, he differentiates among three types of societies, underdeveloped, authoritarian (Communist), and Western democracies, and discusses briefly the factors making for student unrest in each type. Unfortunately, Lipset does not really elaborate his classification or relate the character and structure of student movements to it specifically or systematically. Furthermore, he is essentially concerned with noninstitutionalized forms of student activism and neglects to discuss the relationship between student organizations and the polity in different kinds of societies.

Any analysis of student activism, however, must include this aspect of student life for, as Weinberg and Walker (1969: 80) point out in a recent article that is also critical of the neglect of political variables:

> the form, persistence, and consequences of such issue-oriented [noninstitutionalized] protest movements are significantly affected by the existing structural relations between the university and the state and between student politics and the environing political system at both the local and national levels. An understanding of these effects requires prior analysis of the relationship between these structural arrangements and *institutionalized* forms of student politics, such as student government or the student political party.

They identify two principal variables that shape the character of organized student activism in any society: the degree of government control over higher education, and the pattern of student recruitment to political careers. On the basis of these two variables, they develop a fourfold classification within which they locate four types of organized forms of student politics. Where both government control and recruitment are strong, factional competition among political party branches exist; where both are weak, university student government is strong; where government control is strong and recruitment weak, national student unions are to be found, and where recruitment is strong and government control weak, political clubs are commonly found on campuses. They then test the applicability of this approach in France, Great Britain, the United States, and Latin America, and also assess its implications for noninstitutionalized activism. Although this article, by emphasizing the importance of linkages between students and polity, represents an important pioneering effort, the authors never discuss political system characteristics in a systematic or comprehensive fashion or relate their linkage variables explicitly to this dimension, so that the theoretical basis for the selection of the particular linkage variables is never adequately developed.

Another recent study, by Koplin (1968), that also seeks to develop a conceptual framework for comparative analysis, is more encompassing in scope and more systematic in its consideration of political variables. The author identifies politicization as the dependent variable and discusses specific roles that students may play depending upon their perceptions of the legitimacy of the system. The character of the educational system (elite or mass), the coerciveness of the regime, and the degree of congruity between students and the political elite, constitute the major independent variables. The basis for selecting these dimensions, however, remains unclear, as does their significance, since, in the discussion of each variable, reference is often made to other factors that appear of more basic significance. The character of the educational system, whether it be elite or mass, for example, is emphasized essentially on the grounds that, in the former type, the high student expectations concerning future opportunities will, in fact, be fulfilled. In our view, therefore, expectations of future opportunities as a facet of relative deprivation, and not the character of the educational system, becomes the major independent variable; coercion, however, does represent an important systemic variable to which we shall return below.

From this brief discussion of the literature, it is clear that no comprehensive and systematic framework for the analysis of the phenomenon of student activism has yet been developed. This literature also suggests that three major dimensions must be included in any such framework. Hence, if we regard the frequency and severity of student activism as the dependent variable, all these studies indicate that its alterations are determined by (1) the character of the overall systemic context, particularly the political system; (2) the structure and dynamics of the academic environment, including existing student organizations; and (3) linkage variables that interrelate the two sectors.

Our first dimension, the societal context, refers to the character of the society within which student activism occurs. Although several factors will be discussed, our primary focus will remain upon the political system. Ideology (including religious orientation), and international penetration are environmental variables which set the stage for detailed consideration of the operant functions of the political system itself.

Many attributes of a political system could be singled out for consideration: its degree of differentiation, level of institutionalization, extent of subsystemic autonomy, and the like, but for the analysis of student activism two aspects appear most relevant: the legitimacy of the regime and the degree of its repressive control. These represent our primary independent variables.

Few concepts in the social sciences have received as much attention as legitimacy, and a wide range of scholars have sought to illuminate the causes, character, and results of people's attitudes toward the political system. Analytically, it is possible to distinguish between support for three levels of the polity: the basic community, the particular "rules of the game," and the specific government or occupants of positions who actually formulate and administer policy (Easton, 1965; Goldrich, 1966). It is generally assumed that qualitative differences characterize states that enjoy a high degree of support from their citizens as contrasted with those which are not regarded as worthy of trust and loyalty. Our basic proposition is that, when students identify with the polity at all three levels, little anti-systemic activism will occur. Conversely, if students reject the specific government and the regime as well, activism will be anti-systemic in nature.

Empirical studies which, it should be noted, operationalize "legitimacy" in different and not entirely adequate ways, tend to support this generalization, for it has been demonstrated that legitimacy does inhibit civil strife. The relationship, however, is not clear-cut, and, when societies are classified according to different regime characteristics, important distinctions were uncovered. Legitimacy continues to vary inversely with strife in developing, democratic, and personalist states, but does not do so strongly in the newest, least developed, or authoritarian states (Gurr, 1970: 191-192, 1969: 605-607). These findings are supported and refined by another study which divided conflict into two dimensions, "organized violence" and "anomic violence." The former is marked by organized attempts to achieve such long-term goals as independence or systemic change through guerrilla warfare or revolutionary activities—the latter by spontaneity and disorganization—and includes riots, demonstrations, and strikes.

When legitimacy was correlated with these two forms of violence in Latin America, important variations were exposed. Legitimacy associated highly and negatively with organized violence, but no such association emerged for anomic violence (Bwy, 1971). The specific relationship between legitimacy and the full gamut of student activism (organized and anomic) within Turkey will be a major focus of our analysis.

Our second systemic variable, though widely recognized as important, has received far less attention in the literature. Quite obviously, however, the structure and functioning of student movements varies greatly between democratic and authoritarian societies. Similarly, the perceived risk in sponsoring or participating in a particular event will influence its organization, size, consequences, and the like. Accordingly, we propose that the organization of formal student associations and their activities, as well as the character of noninstitutionalized student activism, will be determined by the degree of repression within the society. Where repression is high, student organizations will be tightly controlled, organized either on a national or a local basis, be closely affiliated with the national political party, be pro-systemic and seek to socialize students in particular; its leaders will consist of present or aspiring government or party officials, and the types of issues with which the organization will be concerned will be academic and student-oriented. Where repression is low, on the other hand, a proliferation of organizations will be evident, and these will reflect the cleavages within the political system. Their goals will be to aggregate and articulate student interests, to influence national politics, and to enhance the power of the parent organization. Leadership will be in the hands of students, though in highly politicized situations, "professional" students will dominate. The character of noninstitutionalized student activism will also be affected by this variable. The greater the level of repression, the more likely that student outbreaks will be spontaneous, sparked by a single crisis, of short duration, of occasional frequency, and of high intensity. Where repression is low, student protests will be planned, of long duration, and will tend to involve representatives of other societal groups.

Empirical studies are also relevant here, for many scholars have examined the relationship between coercion and civil strife. In this area, however, problems of operationalization are even greater than was the case for studies of legitimacy, so that findings can best be considered suggestive. Nevertheless, it does appear that democratic and authoritarian states are both marked by low levels of violence, and that developing nations with middle levels of repressiveness are most prone to civil strife (Feierabend et al., 1969: 660-663). In other words, when control is very high or very low, stability is greatest, when it falls in a middle range, unrest is most prevalent. One explanation that has been advanced for these findings is that such levels of coercion are not sufficiently high to inhibit activism and create a backlash that, in fact, encourages resistance and violence. These studies have led scholars to conclude that the ways in which sanctions are applied may be more significant than the level of control and that the crucial consideration is whether sanctions are consistently applied according to established rules against all offenders (Gurr, 1969: 608-609, 1970: 250 ff.). We shall attempt to assess the degree to which this finding is applicable to student activism in Turkey.

Earlier we noted that many scholars have focused on different aspects of the university environment as the major explanatory variables for student activism, and that any scheme for the analysis of student activism must deal with institutionalized types of student behavior. Accordingly, in our conceptualization, this area, including the student population, the student organizations, and the particular academic environments, represents a discrete subsystem. Within this sector, we shall focus upon the following dimensions which are most commonly discussed in the literature: (1) features of the university environment affecting students; (2) differentiation within the student population; (3) structures and functions of student organizations; and (4) quality and type of student leadership. When analyzing the relationship between these variables and student activism, we shall emphasize their larger political (systemic) significance.

How this sector is linked to the political system and the impact of these interactions upon student activism represents the final dimension of our model. Two specific linkages appear most often in the literature and seem most relevant for comparative analysis: (1) ties between students and other political actors, (2) relative deprivation, especially as manifested in perceptions of future opportunities within the system. The first linkage—the interaction between students and political actors (bureaucratic officials, party leaders, military officers)—has been emphasized by many students of academic unrest in various societies. Exploitation of students by political parties, attempts by regime leaders to utilize students as the carriers of modern ideas to the rest of their traditional society, and the designation of students as scapegoats for particular events, are only a few of the patterns of interaction to be found in the literature. Which of these existed in Turkey and how they relate to targets and levels of student activism and to the primary political variables of legitimacy and repression will be elaborated in our discussion.

Our second linkage—student perceptions of future opportunities as compared to their expectations—has been identified by several scholars as a significant variable affecting political activism. This insight, though never utilized systematically in the literature on student activism, is strongly supported by the extensive work that has been carried out in recent years on political violence. Based on psychological theory, it is not only conceptually exciting and empirically rich, but it provides a theoretical framework within which student activism can be analyzed. Indeed, students are involved in a high percentage of all violence events studied by scholars in this field. Overall, students reportedly participated in 45 percent of all turmoil events, 5 percent of all conspiracies, and 27 percent of all internal wars in 114 polities between 1961 and 1965 (Gurr, 1969; Table 17-7, 589).

The most important work in this field is by Gurr, who has developed a sophisticated theory of political violence. Building on the concept of "relative deprivation," "the actors' perception of discrepancy between their value expectations and their value capabilities" (Gurr, 1970: 24) he has, in his writings, theoretically and empirically investigated the determinants of relative deprivation, the patterns that it takes, the conditions that are necessary for such feelings to be translated into rebellion, and the like. Closely related is the concept of "systemic frustration" (Feierabend et al., 1969) and the "J curve" hypothesis (Davies, 1969). Systemic frustration, which is also based on the agression-frustration hypothesis, translates what is an individual phenomenon to a societal level. It is represented by the formula "social want satisfaction/social want formation" and defined as "frustration that is experienced simultaneously and collectively within societies." The J-curve hypothesis postulates that revolution occurs in societies which experience a sharp setback following an extended period of increasing well-being.

Relative deprivation, however, has been viewed primarily as a prior requisite for unrest. In Gurr's (1969: 596) words: "relative deprivation . . . is a necessary precondition for civil strife of any kind." In our view, student perceptions of their future opportunities within the system is the most salient aspect of relative deprivation and underlies not only their susceptibility to activist behavior but also their valuation of the system and, hence, of its legitimacy. It is in this sense that we view relative deprivation as a linkage variable between the student subsystem and the societal context. In our analysis of student activism in Turkey, however, we shall focus upon both these aspects of relative deprivation.

A schematic representation of our model integrating our various components—systemic context, subsystemic student sector, and linkage variables—is given in Figure 1. Using this framework, we shall organize the available data on student activism in Turkey over time. The narrative will follow well-known historical stages, the nineteenth-century Ottoman Empire, the Young Turk era, and the World War (1908-1922), the Ataturk era and after (1923-1946), the Multi-Party Era (1946-1960), and the decade of the sixties. While tracing the development of the Turkish student movement through these periods, we shall note and discuss the various dimensions of the model presented above. Specifically, we shall assess the extent to which the analysis of political variables furthers our understanding of the characteristic forms of student activism in each particular case. Hopefully, the result will be to refine an approach which may prove of utility in the analysis of student activism on a comparative basis.

THE OTTOMAN EMPIRE

Although the real beginnings of the modern Turkish student movement are to be found in the first decades of the twentieth century, the history of student involvement in political affairs can be traced back at least to the mid-sixteenth century. In those days, higher education was centered in the *Medrese* and possessed a traditional religio-legal orientation. The level of activism of the students at these institutions was apparently quite high, and *softa* riots were commonplace (Akdağ, 1963; Yazici, 1966). In Constantinople in the nineteenth century, for example, incidents occurred in 1853, 1859, and 1876, when theological students were instrumental in causing the downfall of the government and in bringing Midhat Pasha, the great reformer, to power. This episode, however, marked a departure from the previous pattern of softa demonstrations. The difference lay neither in its effectiveness nor in the serious consequences which flowed from it, but in the fact that for the first time a direct link was established between political actors and students. As a struggle raged over the organization of the Empire, 1876 and 1877 were turbulent years—a constitution was proclaimed in 1876—and various political actors took advantage of the existing unrest among the softas to organize them as active demonstrators. This lesson, that students could be mobilized to achieve political

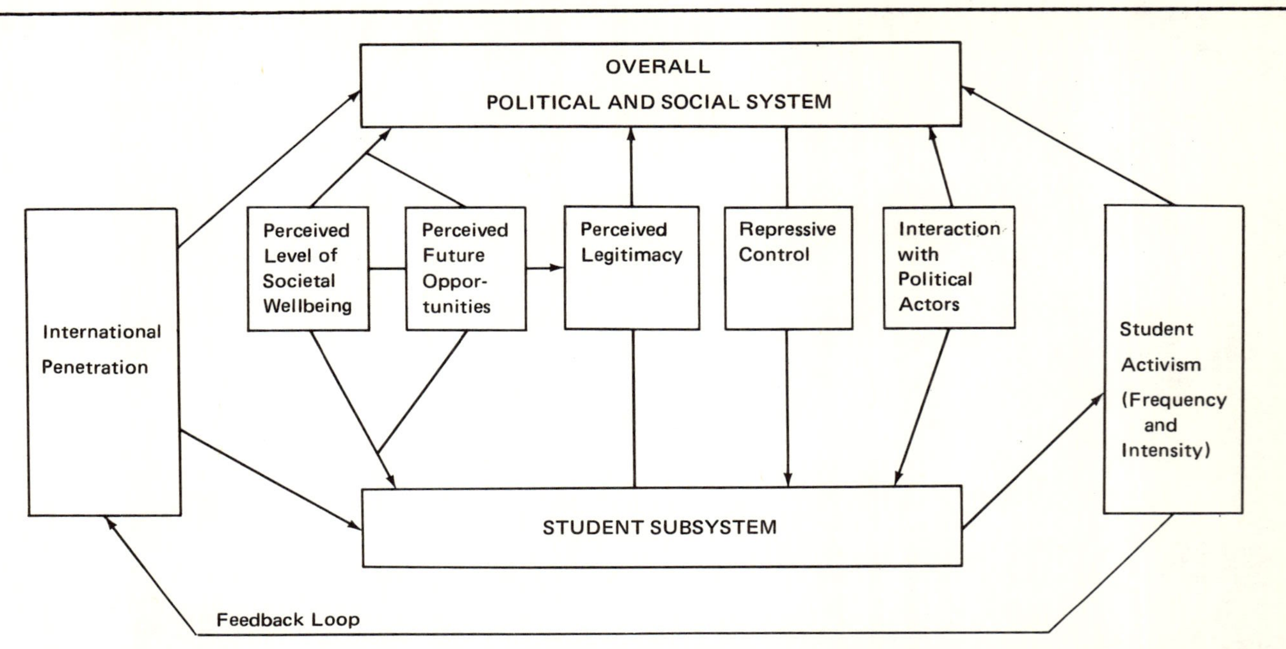

Figure 1: SCHEMATIC OF VARIABLES AFFECTING STUDENT ACTIVISM

objectives, was quickly learned, and it was not long before the tradition was firmly established in all parts of the Middle East (Lewis, 1961: 157).[3]

The willingness of these students to engage in such activism was due, in large part, to the very strong feelings of relative deprivation they experienced. The nineteenth century was marked by a steady deterioration in their position as their numbers increased sharply, while the state became increasingly secularized and one Sultan after another expropriated the revenues of pious foundations. Thus, funds which had been utilized to provide endowments for their support were diverted to other purposes, and, at the same time, future prospects grew increasingly gloomy as the number and types of positions open to them decreased owing to the secularization of the bureaucracy, the judiciary, and the educational system. Affected especially adversely were students of lower-class origin, since those from upper-class families were subsidized and possessed the necessary prerequisites for future success. The mass of the softas, however, who lacked such advantages, tended to view their prospects with dismay as the available channels for occupational and social mobility not only shrank, but became increasingly reserved for those with contacts and influence. Thus, the nineteenth century witnessed the transformation of former centers of intellectual activity into centers of obscurantism inhabited by riffraff, many of whom merely wanted to escape military service. Students such as these were apparently most prone to political agitation (Mardin, 1962: 127-130) and their numbers, estimated at over 30,000 (Ramsaur, 1957: 20 n. 21), made them a formidable force indeed.

The changes which took place during the nineteenth century affected not only the religious students but practically every aspect of Ottoman life and culture. Following a long period of declining power, Ottoman Sultans, particularly Selim III and his successors, came to realize that the very survival of the Ottoman state was at stake, and they sponsored various reforms to strengthen the Empire. At first it was believed that the adoption of Western military techniques would suffice to redress the balance of power with European states, but Ottoman leaders soon realized that the very structure of the Empire had to undergo change, and the organization of a modern military establishment was quickly followed by the reorganization and differentiation of the administration, the adoption cf new legal codes, and the rapid development of a secular educational system. In 1876, the first genuine parliament in Ottoman history was convened, but it proved to be short-lived as Sultan Abdul Hamid II, after ascending the throne, moved quickly to consolidate power in his own hands, suspending the constitution after two years.

Though the Hamidian period was one of political tyranny, the Sultan was not adverse to change, and willingly accepted reforms including the continuing development of a modern educational system, to strengthen the Empire. Somewhat surprisingly, in view of his alertness to possible threats to his power, he did not view the rapid extension of educational opportunities as a danger, and many new technical institutes were opened during his reign to provide the Empire with experts in such fields as administration, veterinary medicine, law, finance, and engineering. Indeed, it was during his reign, as part of the twenty-fifth anniversary celebrations, that the first native university in the Middle East, the *Darülfünun,* was opened in 1900.

The motives that influenced Abdul Hamid II's decision and the measures that he took to minimize the dangers involved reflect quite clearly the highly repressive character of his regime. Three previous attempts to establish a university, in 1846, 1870, and 1879, had been unsuccessful, but by the end of the century the need for university-level training was clearly established. Most importantly, however, the Sultan believed that smaller risks were involved than when students were sent abroad to such centers of revolutionary ideas as Paris for training. To ensure that the students in the new institution would not be corrupted, Abdul Hamid merely applied the same policy that he utilized to prevent any potential or actual threat to his regime from developing anywhere. He extended his extensive and effective spy system to the university and maintained close control over all aspects of university life. No courses on politics or sociology were included in the curriculum of the new institution, inspectors from the Ministry of Education attended classes in order to control the teaching, and the extensive network of spies maintained a close watch over students and faculty. And, to minimize the potential threat from a large concentration of students in Istanbul, the university was small. In 1903, a total of 85 students were enrolled—30 in science, 25 in letters, and 30 in theology (Ergin, 1941: 1002 ff.). Not surprisingly, therefore, the university was of low quality, intellectually passive, and no evidence of any activism among these students is available.

Such passivity was not the case everywhere, for Abdul Hamid's reforms, particularly the growth of railroads and of telegraph communications, spurred the dissemination of new values, concepts, and symbols throughout the Empire. Most affected by these developments were the intellectuals, whose numbers were growing constantly as a result of the continuing expansion of the educational system. Although Abdul Hamid apparently enjoyed the support of the masses the legitimacy of his regime, as far as the intellectuals were concerned, was very low. They felt that the early promise of his reign had never been fulfilled and came increasingly to view the government as corrupt, incompetent, and unresponsive to challenges that were threatening the very existence of the state.

Among the most disaffected groups were the officers in the army and the cadets in the military schools. Abdul Hamid had always been ambivalent about the military. Counterbalancing his desire for a strong military establishment was his fear of revolution. No ammunition, for example, was permitted on board ships which, in any case, were kept anchored in the Golden Horn, out of range of the palace. Similar considerations affected his policy toward the army, and he attempted to establish control over all aspects of military life. As a result, conditions deteriorated greatly. Rank was now determined more than ever, not by achievement, but by influence and favoritism. At the same time, the financial condition of the officer corps was deplorable. Not only was the salary scale relatively low, but pay was usually in arrears, and most officers were forced to discount their income to speculators to maintain themselves and their families. Favoritism was rampant, and promotion was earned, not through achievement, but by personal influence or by becoming an informer on one's fellow officers (Ramsaur, 1957: 16-17).

The cadets in the military schools were, of course, aware of these conditions and were thus subject to strong feelings of relative deprivation and dissatisfaction which affected their view of the regime. Like the softas, though from opposing ideological perspectives, the cadets were unhappy with the status quo and alienated from a government which viewed them with suspicion and prevented them from affecting the destiny of the Empire in the way in which they felt entitled because of their background and training.

As early as 1889, cadets in the military schools were organizing against the regime. In that year, students in the army medical school established a secret society—the Ottoman Society for Union and Progress—and the movement spread rapidly to other higher institutions, particularly the military college and the civil college, although it also had adherents in other higher institutions including the military, veterinary, and engineering schools, the artillery school, and the Naval Academy (Ramsaur, 1957: 17-18; Taylak, 1969: 14 ff.; Tunaya, 1952: 102 ff.). Although the Sultan's spies uncovered this society and broke it up, exiling some of the leaders, imprisoning others, new groups sprang up as opposition continued to grow within the Empire, and Paris and Geneva became centers of exile activity. The military cadets remained in the vanguard of the fight against the regime and various measures adopted by the Sultan, including the expulsion of two classes from the military college, failed to quell the opposition, and the institution remained, according to one author (Orga, 1958: 32), a "hotbed of activity . . . every officer seemed to be a revolutionary." How widespread the discontent was and the extent to which students in the different schools were interacting are indicated by an incident in 1897 when 78 persons were exiled for having affixed posters throughout Istanbul denouncing the Sultan. Of the exiles, 43 were students: 25 from the military medical school, 10 from the military college, 4 from the military engineering school, and one each from military veterinary school, the civilian medical school, an Istanbul lycée, and the military lycée (Taylak, 1969: 24).

Despite such continuing revolutionary activities—in 1902, secret associations existed in the law school and the military college (Taylak, 1969: 34)—the Sultan was able, through his effective policies of control and repression, to prevent any significant threat from emerging until 1908, when the Third Army Corps centered in Salonika revolted, and forced him to restore the constitution of 1876.

Student activism in this period conforms quite closely to our model. Systemic frustration was high, and students at theological and military schools shared similar and equally dismal perceptions of their future opportunities. The religious students, however, were not active after Abdul Hamid came to power, perhaps because of his emphasis upon Pan Islam and his attempt to strengthen his position by manipulating religious symbols. Whatever the reason, the religious students never organized themselves as did the military cadets who were in touch with a variety of revolutionary groupings in the Empire and abroad. Their activism was also shaped extensively by the character of the political system at this time. Only during its early years did the Hamidian regime enjoy any legitimacy among the educated elements; by the late 1880s, the legitimacy of the regime had sunk so low that revolutionary activity was under way among students, and Abdul Hamid was able to retain power only through the application of a high degree of repression—though it should be noted that repression in the nineteenth-century Ottoman Empire meant exile and not execution. Nevertheless, in this hostile environment, open organization was precluded, as were such tactics as demonstrations, meetings, and the like, and the cadets engaged in secret, revolutionary activity.

THE YOUNG TURKS AND WORLD WAR I

The Young Turk revolution of 1908 was greeted with great joy throughout the Empire, but the high expectations that it aroused among Ottomans of all backgrounds were never fulfilled. Elections for a new Ottoman parliament were held in 1908, but the attempt to establish democratic processes collapsed in the face of powerful external threats that embroiled the Empire in one war after another as well as internal challenges from a wide variety of groups. The Committee of Union and Progress (CUP) soon established dictatorial control and remained in power, except for a short period in 1912-1913, through World War I.

The achievements of the Young Turks in the face of the extraordinary difficulties with which they had to deal should not be underestimated, for they adopted important reform policies, particularly after 1913, in such fields as education, women's rights, law, local administration, economic development, and culture that spurred the transformation of Ottoman society and laid the basis for the emergence of the Turkish Republic. As part of these reforms, the Darülfünun was reorganized and expanded. It was moved to a new location with more adequate facilities, the curriculum was completely revised, and the medical and law faculties were integrated into the institution. The number of applicants increased sharply, as did the number of students, who numbered 4,380 by 1910. Of these, 2,500 were studying law; 850, medicine (Mears, 1924: 125), but little additional information is available concerning the student body other than the fact that of 1,808 students reportedly enrolled in the law school in 1913-1914, 41 percent were the sons of bureaucrats, 13 percent of merchants, 7 percent of religious leaders, 3 percent of teachers, 3 percent of artisans, and 4 percent of farmers (Ergin, 1941: 917).[4]

Moreover, the Young Turk era was one of constant intellectual ferment and was marked, particularly in its early period, by intensive political activity. The first heady months after the revolution witnessed a remarkable proliferation of associations, clubs, factions, and groupings, and a considerable degree of political involvement by students who formed several organizations, held meetings and demonstrations, and issued communiques on various issues and in support of specific political actors (Taylak, 1969: 50-67). Following the abortive counter-revolution in March 1909 on behalf of Sultan Abdul Hamid in which softas were involved, however, a marked shift within the polity occurred as the CUP emerged as the dominant political force and established its control over all aspects of political life. Thereafter, the students remained relatively quiescent until after 1911, when discontent with Young Turk policies was openly articulated and the Liberals came to power for a brief period. In October 1912, Darülfünun students demonstrated several times in favor of war, and the following January students were involved in the coup d'état which restored the Committee of Union and Progress to power (Taylak, 1969: 79 ff.).

In these years, ideological questions assumed a hitherto unknown significance as students and intellectuals debated the structure of the Empire and its future shape with a hitherto unknown scope and intensity. Some felt that it should remain a multiracial, multinational Empire; others that it should be a centralized state wherein Turks were dominant. Although the latter view, espoused by the CUP, soon became policy, there was no consensus as to how the serious problems confronting the state should be resolved. Essentially, three main currents competed for acceptance: the Islamist, the Westernist, and the Turkist, each with a different perspective toward change and innovation (see Berkes, 1964: 333 ff.). The Islamists rejected and opposed modernization, and although the Westernists and the Turkists agreed on the necessity for drastic change, they disagreed upon the extent to which Western institutions should be adopted, and upon the role that Islam should play within the society. The Westernists advocated total acceptance of European values, culture, and technology, and favored a secular state.

The leading Turkist theoretician and one of the great Turkish intellectuals of modern times was Ziya Gökalp, a prominent member of the Young Turk movement who was elected to the Central Committee in 1909. He argued that the basic element of a nation was its culture, which had to be preserved and maintained above all; only the material and technological aspects of Europe should be adopted, and even these only after the country had sufficiently developed its own culture based upon the Turkish heritage, so that its Turkish character would not be affected by innovations. He favored a secular state, but since he considered Islam an integral part of the national culture, he felt it should play an important role in every person's life. The nation was the highest moral authority, and the intelligentsia were the natural leaders of the nation.

This resumé represents an oversimplification, since Gökalp was not a consistent ideologue and modified his views rather sharply throughout his life in light of political, social, and personal developments. In fact, one of his disciples once complained that because Gökalp "was always changing the fundamental elements of the national ego; they could never be definite for fear they might be called on to formulate something quite different on the same subject" (Edip, 1926: 384). Nevertheless, his ideas were extremely influential and can be exemplified by his famous slogan: "We belong to the Turkish nation, the Muslim religious community, and the European civilization."

Many intellectuals and students, both civilian and military, were followers of Gökalp, and, in 1911, 190 students at the military medical school published a letter in which they stressed the need to revitalize and develop the Turkish nation and suggested the creation of a nonpolitical organization to achieve these goals. This suggestion was readily accepted by the members of the *Türk Derneği* (Turkish Association), established soon after the 1908 revolution by Gökalp and his followers who joined with the students to organize the *Türk Ocaklari* (Turkish Hearths). In 1915, Gökalp, who was not only active in the Türk Ocaklari but also served as director of the party's youth department, was appointed Professor of Sociology at the Darülfünun, and his influence upon students was enhanced even more.[5] In 1916, a university student organization, which was to be the nucleus of Milli Türk Talebe Birliği (MTTB; National Turkish Student Association) was established. It possessed a highly nationalist and Turkist orientation, an orientation that was to endure for many years and, as we shall see, profoundly affected developments during the Ataturk era.

It is difficult, however, to assess the degree to which student activism in this period conforms to our model, since few data on such variables as relative deprivation or legitimacy are available. It appears likely, however, that legitimacy was quite high during World War I and, even before, for the era was a turbulent one marked by a series of almost constant challenges to the very survival of the Empire and by change and innovation in many fields. Thus, though no unanimity existed on questions of domestic or foreign policy, feelings of patriotism were quite marked (Emin, 1914: 107), and such feelings may well have countervailed feelings of deprivation created by the prospect of military service confronting most students. Whether this was indeed the case deserves further research, but it must be remembered that the political system was repressive and opportunities for activism limited. It is not by chance that students were active during periods of political turmoil when control and repression were low. Most incidents involving students occurred in the early days of the revolutionary era, and there is little evidence of student activism when the CUP had consolidated its power.

The strength of patriotic feelings among the students and the degree to which repression affects activism is also evidenced by events following the 1918 armistice when students joined with other groups, intellectuals, veterans, and officers, to protest the allied occupation and the Greek invasion of Anatolia. Meetings were organized in the Darülfünun as well as large rallies in public squares at which various nationalist leaders were invited to speak by the student organizers. Such activities were not tolerated for long by the occupying powers, and press censorship and other effective measures soon suppressed them. Nevertheless, student activism in support of the nationalist movement continued, though in a different form. Although some students escaped to Anatolia to join the forces of Mustapha Kemal, those who remained in Istanbul engaged in such activities as distributing handbills, affixing posters, and smuggling arms (Taylak, 1969: 90 ff.; Ariburnu, 1951). Thus, in a period marked by high repression and low legitimacy, students engaged in organized, secret anti-systemic activity, as they had done in the days of Abdul Hamid II.

THE ONE-PARTY ERA (1923-1946)

The establishment of the Turkish Republic and the emergence of Mustapha Kemal as a great charismatic leader was accompanied by a resurgence of student activism. The Darülfünun Student Association was established in 1923, and shortly thereafter the national organization (MTTB) was formed so as to include students in various higher institutes. MTTB quickly emerged into national prominence. It called for a boycott of the Belgian company (Sofina) running Istanbul's tramway to protest against the company's refusal to give students discounts. The campaign quickly gained widespread support and a protest demonstration to publicize the issue culminated in the wrecking of the company's central offices and the wounding of two students by police. While the resulting investigation was under way, another incident occurred. This time a disturbance broke out at a party honoring visiting Roumanian students, and, because a Dutch official was involved as a victim, the press condemned the students (Taylak, 1969: 107). Despite such disapproval, however, one result of these two events was to strengthen the student organization, whose popularity and influence rose among the students. A second result, however, was to alarm the government, which decided to take various steps to control the students. Its first reaction, following the tramway incident, had been one of concern for the students' financial plight. Feeling that the underlying cause for the event was student poverty, some funds were made available to the students, but these were apparently appropriated by activists. Soon thereafter, however, the government changed its policy. The young, progressive rector who had been sympathetic to the students resigned, and a new set of regulations was formulated and enforced within the faculties. Moreover, the government decided to bring the student organization completely under its influence; it enrolled some CHP members as students and sought, unsuccessfully, to elect them to office (Taylak, 1969: 106-107).

These repressive measures, however, and the high legitimacy that the new government enjoyed, resulted in a period of quiet. For several years, the students concerned themselves only with their own problems and with maintaining ties with student organizations abroad. The strength of MTTB declined drastically, and the organization was apparently in danger of dissolution by 1928 (Taylak, 1969: 108).

The character, intensity, and type of student activism in the twenties, therefore, reflect the character of the political system—high repression and high legitimacy. The target of student activism was not a domestic political actor but a foreign company which was accused of continuing exploitative practices. Moreover, although the government reacted strongly, its measures did not lead to any other activism or affect the students' perceptions of the legitimacy of Mustapha Kemal's administration. In 1928, for example, during an excursion in front of Ataturk's residence, the students erupted into cheers (Taylak, 1969: 111).

Of course, there was little incentive for student unrest during this period. Though many students may have been poor, the decade of the twenties was a revolutionary era for Turkey. Following his victory over the Greek armies, Mustapha Kemal almost overnight began to modernize the nation. The Sultanate and the Caliphate were abolished, and a secular republic established; the power of the theocracy was broken, and traditional ways of thinking and acting were shattered as one dramatic reform followed another in rapid succession, including the outlawing of the fez, the adoption of the Gregorian calendar, the romanization of the alphabet, and the replacement of Islamic law by Western legal codes. Not only were the students caught up in these stirring events, but they were singled out for special attention by Ataturk, who was most conscious of the necessity to create a new elite if his revolution was to succeed: an elite that could only come from the institutions of higher learning. In fact, Ataturk specifically entrusted the future of the nation to the youth, both in his Bursa speech and in the peroration to his famous Seven Day Speech in October 1927, which every Turkish youth learns by heart. Ataturk declared, "Turkish youth! Your primary duty is ever to preserve and defend the national independence, the Turkish Republic. That is the only basis of your existence and your future" (Kemal, 1929: 723).

In this heady atmosphere, it was natural for students to regard Ataturk as a great dynamic leader who was forging a powerful modern state out of the ashes of a moribund and obsolete empire and to accord high legitimacy to the political system. Moreover, feelings of relative deprivation were practically nonexistent, as Ataturk was promising and making it possible for students to achieve positions of leadership and prominence within the new nation.

In the late twenties, however, conditions changed drastically within Turkey, and discontent with the government and its policies became more and more evident. Though the Ataturk regime was a dictatorship, it was never cruel or tyrannical, and a considerable amount of freedom of expression was permitted. Now a series of bad harvests, coupled with a lack of economic development, fed increasing resentment against the government and its policies; the onset of the world depression in 1929 further aggravated the situation and had a profound impact upon student perceptions of future opportunities and, indeed, upon their immediate circumstances. Unfortunately, few data are available concerning the composition of the student body at this time, but the two largest faculties were still law, with 1,278 students, and medicine, with 884 students (Devlet İstatistik Enstitusu, 1967: 66), which explains the preponderance of activists from those two faculties. Furthermore, it is likely that the great majority came from urban middle-class backgrounds, and that many were the sons of government officials, as had always been the case. This group, whose numbers had increased sharply during the twenties, suffered great hardships during the depression as the government was forced to make sizable cuts in its budget, 34% of which went, in 1930, for civil service salaries (Hershlag, 1960: 85). Those students who supported themselves by working were also affected as the depression threw many people out of work, and as the opportunities for government employment, the principal source of student positions (Toynbee and Kirkwood, 1927: 247-248), was greatly curtailed. Accordingly, it appears that, as in the nineteenth century, one of the major underlying reasons for the restlessness of the students was their depressed position and their high level of relative deprivation. Now it was difficult to stay in school, and their prospects were very different from those of earlier graduates. No longer were they assured an important role in the nation's life, a role that they had been taught by Ataturk himself to regard as their right, and it is likely that this realization was an important factor making for the resurgence of student activism.

This resurgence took place in a period of ideological and political ferment, as the debate which had been taking place within the country about Ataturk's policies intensified and gained added ideological dimensions. For some time, opposition to specific policies had been voiced by many intellectuals, some of whom were Marxists, others of whom felt that he was going too fast and destroying a valuable heritage. Reinforcing this debate were developments in the USSR, Nazi Germany, and Fascist Italy, for the ferment within the country was deeply shaped by international penetration. As conditions deteriorated economically, more and more attention was paid to the ways in which totalitarian states were organizing their societies, and anti-Western and nationalist feelings rose significantly in the late twenties and early thirties.

Students were not immune to these ideological currents, and fascism, communism, pan-Turanism, and Islamic reaction all enjoyed support in varying degrees within the university (Taylak, 1969: 110; Genç, 1971: 13). Uniting most students, however, was a strong feeling of nationalism. Thus, the first manifestation of renewed student activism took the shape of a campaign by the Law Faculty Organization stressing the use of Turkish by all citizens, including minorities, and the following year, in 1929, MTTB started to promote the purchase of Turkish goods (Taylak, 1969: 111).

MTTB appears to have been strongly influenced by the philosophy of Ziya Gökalp, who, despite official downgrading of his importance following his death in 1924, remained influential, especially among those active in the Türk Ocaklari and within the Darülfünun, where many of his followers were on the faculty. This is clearly reflected in the controversy that erupted around a new publication, *Resimli Ay,* which had been started by Nazim Hikmet, the noted leftist poet, following his return from Moscow in 1928. It focused upon the social and economic problems of Turkey, but soon Hikmet began a campaign against the more conservative elements of the Turkish press. A second target was the Türk Ocaklari. MTTB reacted strongly to these attacks. It held a meeting in 1929 in the course of which "the efforts of the Bolsheviks to poison the country's youth in the Darülfünun" were discussed. It was decided that students would visit the papers that were being attacked to indicate their respect for the journalists involved and would also visit Hikmet's offices to express their indignation at the attacks against Türk Ocaklari.

This incident demonstrates the degree to which Ziya Gökalp's philosophy—which, as we have noted, ran counter to Ataturk's conception of modernization and secular nationalism in significant ways—remained influential within the university. On the other hand, its aftermath demonstrates the degree of ideological ferment among the students. Law students opposed the action of MTTB and held an extraordinary meeting to discuss the matter, in the course of which they denounced both the leftists and the conservatives. A subsequent meeting, in which students from all faculties were represented, witnessed criticism of MTTB and the resignation of its president (Taylak, 1969: 113 ff.).

Such dissension was not limited to students, but characterized the political system at this time. How widespread the unrest was became obvious in 1930 when Ataturk permitted trusted associates to establish an opposition party, a bold experiment which reflected his genuine commitment to democratic processes. The result, however, was not the hoped for gradual evolution of a loyal and responsible opposition, but a direct challenge to Ataturk's position as dissidents and opponents in all sectors of the society quickly flocked to the banner of the Liberal Party. Ataturk reacted quickly and firmly and, within a short period, closed the organization. Student activism also came to an abrupt, though temporary, halt.

This disastrous attempt to increase popular participation brought into focus the need for additional reforms if the new Turkey were to become a permanent creation, and soon after, Ataturk inaugurated fundamental changes in many aspects of educationan and intellectual life. The great educational reforms which were promulgated in the 1930s—the closing of the Türk Ocaklari and of the Darülfünun, and their replacement with a network of People's Houses and a modern university respectively, and the new efforts at expanding education at the lower levels—were designed to raise the level of the mass, close the elite-mass gap, and to create a modern, Westernized elite that shared Ataturk's philosophy.

Ataturk moved first against the Türk Ocaklari, which he regarded as a possible rival organization to the CHP (Republican People's Party) and as centers for the dissemination of a philosophy which conflicted to a considerable extent, with his own views. Indeed, many members had flocked to the banner of the Liberal Party (Taylak, 1969: 75). As early as 1927, the CHP had decided to extend its control over the organization; now it was officially closed. Two years later he struck a second major blow at conservative institutions when he replaced the Darülfünun with Istanbul University. For years, discontent with the poor academic reputation of the institution, its notorious cleavages and feuds, and its conservative orientation, had been quite widespread. Little if any research was carried out by the faculty, many of whom maintained low professional standards. Appointments were made not on the basis of ability, but were often the result of personal intrigues. At the same time, many faculty were opposed to various aspects of Ataturk's reforms; their conservatism is indicated by the fact that professors had condemned students who had their pictures taken and had fought against the latinization of the alphabet (Başgöz and Wilson, 1968: 61, 85).

The change was far more than one of mere nomenclature. The entire faculty was dismissed, and only 59 out of 151 professors, those who knew foreign languages and who had demonstrated scholarly competence, were rehired. Vacancies were filled with foreign professors, especially refugees from Germany, and, within a short period, far higher standards were achieved in the university than had ever been the case before. To ensure that the university would function in the expected manner, vastly expanded resources were allocated to it—its budget in 1934 was double that of 1931—(Bilsel, 1943) and the previous policy of autonomy was replaced by one of strict government control. Several new institutes were created to encourage research on contemporary issues, and, to ensure that students would now be exposed to appropriate political socialization, the most important of these institutes, on the history of the Turkish revolution, offered compulsory courses.

It was at this time of economic difficulty and social and political change that the most intensive period of student activism occurred. Suddenly and unexpectedly, within the space of two months, the students staged two major demonstrations involving thousands of people, and MTTB began to enjoy a period of remarkable national prominence. It held regular meetings, sponsored various campaigns, engaged in public debates with various groups and government officials and, since students were "without a tongue," published a newspaper, *Birlik*. The first incident occurred on February 25, 1933, when students gathered on the campus to protest the firing of a Turkish employee by the Wagon-Lits Company for refusing to comply with a directive to speak French during business hours. The students soon decided to march on the company, and, having equipped themselves with stones on the way, they smashed the windows of the company's offices. Upon running out of ammunition, they proceeded to tear up the street for missiles. The speeches which preceded the rioting revealed that, although the Wagon-Lits Company was the primary target, there was a deep feeling among these students against all stores and agencies with foreign names. The crowd, which numbered several thousand, was eventually dispersed; several students were arrested, but all were later released.

On April 30, the students staged another demonstration, this time to protest the desecration of a Turkish cemetery in Razgrad, Bulgaria. The incident revealed a marked degree of independence by the students, for, following news of the event in Bulgaria, MTTB called a meeting to decide how to react. Officials told the students that the affair was the government's responsibility, and the governor of Istanbul denied their application for a permit to demonstrate. The students decided to defy this order. They gathered in front of the Bulgarian Consulate, marched to the Bulgarian cemetery located nearby in order to place flowers on the graves—a demonstration to the world of the higher level of civilization of Turkish students. They they marched to Taksim, one of the main squares of Istanbul, but police attempted to halt the parade with predictable results. Eighty students were arrested, and the government issued an order closing MTTB.[6]

Once again MTTB defied the government. They responded by sending letters to Ataturk himself as well as to the Prime Minister, the Minister of Education, and the General Secretary of the CHP, in which they declared their innocence, and to the Minister of Interior appealing the decision to close the organization. Moreover, an extraordinary meeting was convened in the university attended by 51 MTTB delegates and about 100 students to discuss the telegram that they had received from Ataturk in which he pointedly remarked:

> It is one of our most important concerns that the youth be raised as hardworking, conscientious, and nationalistic. Youth must be careful in carrying out all its activities to obey the laws of the Republic and the rules and principles of the agents of the Republic. You can be sure that the government recognizes its duties in the face of national problems and that the judicial powers of the country are fair and just [Vakit, 1933; Taylak, 1969: 129].

Subsequently, 23 MTTB leaders and members of the executive committee were released from jail. The remaining 57 were not pardoned until January 1934, but MTTB was apparently permitted to continue its activities (Taylak, 1969: 130).

The degree to which the ideological orientation of MTTB activists remained Turkist, nationalist, and anti-Western is evidenced not only by the character of the incidents but also from an examination of the contents of its newspaper, *Birlik,* and the minutes of the MTTB's executive committee.[7] Its program was defined in the minutes as including the following: "A Turkism which first focuses upon the Turks within the national boundary, and after that reaches to Turks living outside" and "struggles against all cosmopolitan understandings that threaten Turkish culture: fashion, language, foreign schools, movies, and movie magazines."

Before long the emblem of the Grey Wolf, with its Turkist connotation, was adopted by MTTB as its official symbol. Several motifs run through the paper, including a concern with foreign penetration as evidenced by opposition to the West, especially to foreign institutions active in Turkey, an identification with Turks throughout the world, attempts to arouse pride in national symbols and to prevent their abuse, and a concern, albeit limited, with student affairs. Specific articles decried the neglect of the Turkish flag, attacked shops with foreign names, foreign schools, minorities, Masons, Communists, and the YMCA, demanded respect for the national anthem, deplored the condition of the Turks in Central Asia, urged the need for rural development, demanded cheaper tramway fares, and opened a campaign to erect an appropriate monument to commemorate the Turkish victory at Çannakale (Gallipoli) during World War I. Two quotations will serve to convey the flavor of *Birlik's* contents. The first, which appeared in the issue of August 2, 1933, states:

> There are three enemies, black, red, white. The priest, sometimes he looks like an American sportsman . . . the Communists, who call a Jewish philosopher with a long beard prophet, [and] heroin.

The second, from almost the last issue, July 2, 1934, is as follows:

> We are nationalists. We are not a nation for exploitation, we can never be and we shall never be exploited. We are extreme nationalists. The nation according to us is a society of people who have the same blood, culture, and goals. For us nationalism knows no boundaries. Turks living in the Crimea, Samarkand . . . do not live within our boundaries but they are part of us. The national character according to us is a spirit which holds Turkey superior over all nations . . . which fights against the denial of the past and of Turkish customs and has respect for the Great Turks.

These attitudes brought MTTB into conflict with *Kadro*, a magazine representing a new sociopolitical philosophy that had emerged in Turkey. Combining elements of Marxism and fascism, the magazine argued that an elite had to lead Turkey to economic development and that the state which represented all classes would play the dominant role in this effort (Karpat, 1959: 70 ff.). In various articles discussing the two incidents and students in general, *Kadro* charged irresponsibility and lack of discipline, and argued that although the youth of Turkey sought to play an active role in the country's development, it did not know how to do so meaningfully. It suggested that students learn the principles of the Turkish revolution and commit themselves to its achievement. *Birlik* responded bitterly to these attacks, asserting its independence and stating "Turkish youth is not a parrot. It does not have to memorize the principles of the Turkish revolution because they [sic] know them as well as anybody" (Taylak, 1969: 141).

That *Kadro*'s views were shared by the government is evidenced not only by the fact that the CHP officially adopted the principles of revolutionary change, but also by the decision of the government shortly after this interchange with *Kadro* to repress the students. In August 1934, *Birlik* was closed on the grounds that it had dealt with political issues. Although the students denied that they had published political articles and their leaders were optimistic that the government would back down—the minutes of the executive committee included an entry dated August 18, 1934, stating that "The Executive board is sure that this action will be rectified"—it never did, and the paper was to remain closed for many years.

The shifts in the government's policy toward MTTB reflected Ataturk's ambivalent attitudes toward the students. On the one hand, he viewed their ability to mobilize the populace and their willingness to engage in mass demonstrations with concern and disapproval, particularly since their ideological perspectives differed from his own. On the other, he regarded the students as one of the pillars of the new Turkey he was trying to create and was willing to tolerate the existence of MTTB as long as it enjoyed what he regarded to be responsible leadership, and did not overstep the boundaries of criticism and opposition which existed within Turkish society at this time. Nevetheless, to minimize the implicit danger, he kept a close watch on the organization's activities through informants and undercover agents, and as MTTB became more and more outspoken and its views diverged increasingly from his principles and policies, he intervened so as to limit MTTB's ability to influence public opinion. Doubtless, he hoped that the closing of the paper and the ban on public meetings and demonstrations would serve as a warning, and that MTTB would mend its ways.

These repressive measures did prove highly effective and severely damaged the organization. It lost its former momentum and was no longer able to generate the enthusiasm and excitement of previous years. Moreover, financial assistance was no longer forthcoming and, because the legitimacy of the regime remained high, many students, especially the more able ones, were reluctant to associate themselves with an organization so obviously out of favor with the administration. Hence, the quality of the society and of its leadership declined rapidly until the few remaining activists decided that if MTTB were to survive it needed the kind of enthusiasm and support it had enjoyed in 1933. It was agreed to hold a meeting on the Hatay issue in 1936, but the government refused to grant permission. The students decided to ignore the ban; if they were successful, MTTB might be revitalized; if the government took strong measures, they had little to lose. This time the official reaction was swift and definite. The police broke up the meeting and MTTB was officially closed, the Minister of Interior declaring, "The Republican government never tolerated this type of activity by MTTB. Such meetings with students and professors are considered as impediments to the cultural progress of the country" (Taylak, 1969: 155).

Despite its brief and meteoric existence, MTTB had an important impact upon Turkish society. Although not more than two or three hundred students were actively involved in the organization's affairs and only about twelve to fifteen were really influential, it is surprising how many of this inner circle went on to achieve prominence in intellectual and political life. The most obvious examples are Tevfik İleri, Bahadin Dülger, Cihad Baban, and Nihat Erim, all of whom have served as deputies or ministers.

They were not to be followed by other student leaders for many years, for the period of quiet which followed these events lasted through World War II and was marked by an absence of activism. During those years, students had little choice; the government was highly repressive and maintained firm control over all organizations. In 1941, the Minister of Education did grant permission for a student association to be established within Istanbul University, and soon after in the other universities, but the organizations remained under strict faculty and government supervision. Several efforts by the students to obtain independence were unsuccessful and, in these years, student activities were confined to immediate, academically related issues. The association sponsored discussions, debates, sports events, field trips, and celebrated national holidays appropriately.

Thus, the character of student activism between 1923 and 1946 again conforms quite closely to our model. The political system could be described as possessing high legitimacy and medium to high repressive characteristics. Student activism did not occur in periods of high repression and, because of continuing high legitimacy, Ataturk's decisions to repress student activism on various occasions achieved the desired results. Moreover, it is significant that the periods of activism occurred when students seemed to be subject to strong feelings of relative deprivation. Not only were they suffering economically, but the structure of future opportunities had changed drastically by the early thirties. Nevertheless, it is not clear how this condition affected the students' perceptions of regime legitimacy. In our model we postulated a relationship between relative deprivation and legitimacy, but little evidence is available to assess this relationship in the early thirties. It seems as though legitimacy was unaffected, although it should be noted that the students in this period were far more assertive and independent than they had been in earlier years.

THE MULTI-PARTY ERA (1946-1960)

The end of the war inaugurated a period of swift and sudden change within the country. The traditional elite splintered into various factions, and new groups that emerged in the Ataturk era—businessmen, traders, and entrepreneurs—began to articulate ever more insistent demands for a greater role within the polity. In their drive for more power, they quickly gained the support of many elements within the society who, dissatisfied with the rigidity of the CHP, the bureaucracy in general, the war time economic difficulties, and their consequences in particular, wished to see a greater degree of freedom within the country. For many reasons, including President İsmet İnönü's dedication to Ataturk's ideal of establishing a multiparty system, internal dissension within the CHP, and strong demands for an end to one-party rule, opposition parties were legalized. The most important of the opposition parties that emerged was the Democrat Party (DP), formed by four former leaders of the CHP.

In this newly liberalized atmosphere, ideological attitudes ranging from racialism to communism were soon expressed openly, and criticism of the specific actors and policies, particularly the CHP, rose quickly in amount and intensity. The administration reacted to these attacks and, motivated partly by the deterioration of Soviet-Turkish relations that ensued when the USSR made territorial demands upon Turkey, sponsored a demonstration by Istanbul University students on December 4, 1945, that wrecked several publishing houses and distributors (Karpat, 1959: 149 ff.; Taylak, 1969: 175 ff.).

The close ties that existed between political actors and the students were further reinforced the following year when many of the same students reestablished MTTB. They regarded the new organization as a continuation of the MTTB of the thirties and asked for, and received, the assistance of MTTB alumni. The first issue of its journal, *Yeni Milli Birlik*, was numbered "fifteen" since the original *Birlik* had appeared fourteen times. Like its predecessor, this MTTB was from the outset concerned with national political issues, though this time it acted with the blessing of the government, which wanted to gain support and sympathy among the youth and to utilize students for its own political advantage at a time when it was entering a new and unknown era. One representative of the CHP who was concerned with student affairs told the author, "Of course I organized MTTB and I'm proud of it. Look at the results."

Echoing the government position, MTTB took a strong nationalist and anti-Communist line and appointed itself a leader in the fight against communism. In the first issue of its paper, which appeared on December 15, 1949, it warned that Communist newspapers and magazines were infiltrating various institutions, including the educational system, stating, "It is the day to save the youth from the Marxist teachers." It added, "If MTTB had not been closed red propaganda would not have found proper conditions in order to thrive."

To counter this "propaganda," MTTB sought to arouse public opinion through various means including public meetings, debates, discussions, and the like. In 1947, they broke up a meeting at which a "leftist" professor was supposed to lecture, to prevent him from "disseminating communist propaganda," an incident which culminated in the dismissal of four faculty members accused of being Communists from Ankara University, and, in the forced resignation, following student threats, of the dean of the university (Karpat, 1959: 372-373).

Despite the publicity that MTTB gained through these actions, the organization remained small and its base of support limited. In fact, most of its members came, not from regular university faculties, but from various higher institutes. Moreover, because of its highly politicized character, MTTB attracted a particular type of student—those who were interested in a political career. Indeed, MTTB proved to be a valuable school for aspiring politicians, and a remarkable number of its leaders chose to stay in office for several years while developing necessary contacts and awaiting an appropriate moment to move into a political party. A remarkable number of MTTB officers acted in this manner and went on into public life, most as members of the CHP; two obvious examples are Suphi Baykam and Hudai Oral.

No such linkage with the political system characterized the other national student organization which emerged in these years. Known as

Türk Milli Talebe Federasyon (TMTF), it was an outgrowth of the student organizations which had developed within each faculty in the late 1940s. Because of its firm roots within the universities, the high caliber of its leaders, and its genuine attempts to deal with student problems, TMTF from the outset proved to be a much stronger organization than MTTB. In sharp contrast to the practice of MTTB leaders, no TMTF president served more than one term and no TMTF leader from this period entered political life.

Although TMTF was always an independent organization without direct ties to any political actors, it soon found itself involved in political affairs as well as student and campus problems. Its leaders became increasingly concerned with national issues and began to express their views on many of the same subjects that were of concern to MTTB. On various occasions, it joined with the other organization in sponsoring meetings and demonstrations that were anti-Communist in orientation. From 1948 onward, however, this topic declined rapidly in importance; the last incident occurred in 1950 when MTTB and TMTF sponsored a demonstration protesting the release of Nazim Hikmet, the well-known Communist poet, from prison.

It was not this fact that made 1950 such a milestone in Turkey's history. In that year, the Democrat Party (DP) swept into power with an overwhelming majority of the popular vote, an election result which represented a remarkable transition from dictatorship to democracy. In the first free elections in Turkey's history, all segments of society united to voice their dissatisfaction with the CHP, which had been in power for 27 long years—intellectuals demanded freedom; businessmen, an end to etatism; landowners, the status quo; and the peasantry which felt neglected and abused wanted roads, drinking water, and mosques. Secure in its mandate, the DP attempted to carry out its campaign promises. It launched an ambitious program of economic development, financed in large part by U.S. aid, and liberalized various restrictive laws. Aware of the importance of rural support, the DP did its utmost to maintain the favor of the villagers in a variety of ways including, most importantly, the further easing of religious restrictions. Prior to the 1950 elections, the CHP had also relaxed certain controls over religion; now the DP government permitted the call to prayer to be once again chanted in Arabic, and religious instruction became a regular school subject unless the parents formally objected. These changes, which were most popular, also led to a revival and an increase in reactionary activities which greatly disturbed all the modern elements in Turkey. TMTF and MTTB became preoccupied with this issue and made frequent strong statements condemning all reactionary manifestations.

The second important issue on which the student organizations and the government held conflicting views was the question of Cyprus. From 1948 on, both MTTB and TMTF had expressed grave concern over the future of the island and, in the early 1950s, TMTF had organized a Cyprus Committee to focus on this question, even though the Turkish government maintained steadfastly that no real problem existed. Nevertheless, TMTF continued to hold meetings and to issue statements and was, to a considerable extent, responsible for arousing public opinion on this topic. In 1955, the government changed its position and, following the failure to reach an agreement with Greece, organized the demonstrations which degenerated into the riots of September 6-7. Several TMTF leaders who had arranged the original meeting were arrested and two were jailed in the aftermath of these events, as the government used the students as scapegoats.

Even though TMTF found itself speaking out increasingly on what it considered to be urgent matters of national concern, it did so reluctantly, and its leaders always felt that the organization should be concerned primarily with student and university problems. The position of MTTB, on the other hand, was that students had a definite responsibility as an educated and progressive elite to be outspoken on national issues, especially since Ataturk himself had entrusted the youth with this responsibility.

The hesitancy and misgivings with which TMTF became concerned with national problems—and the consequences—are clearly reflected by the comments of a former president, who wrote in its paper:

> During my tenure reactionary activities began in the country. Thereupon it was proposed that TMTF open a campaign against such events. It was pointed out that reaction was as dangerous for our country as communism and even more dangerous [sic]. This action was applauded by most of the press. . . . We were supported from every side of the country. . . . The government worried about this situation . . . they began to shrink from TMTF and they began to apply pressure by saying that the student organization is engaged in politics. . . . The Federation is a student organization. Its basic aims are the needs of the students. But must the Federation struggle with currents that threaten the revolution? If it does, is it moving away from its aims? We struggled when I was president. But from time to time I worried that this struggle was far removed from the basic aims of the Federation. However, when I left . . . student life, I found the opportunity to think soundly. . . . At that time I reached the

opinion that our activity was not wrong and that it was useful for the country. My dear brothers, do not deviate even one centimeter from your activites and your issues [İnkilap Gençliği, 1952].

As a result of its stand, TMTF found itself engaged in a bitter struggle with the *Türk Milliyetciler Derneği,* an extremist organization with a Turkist and pan-Turanist orientation that enjoyed the support of some highly placed persons within the DP including Tevfik İleri, who had been one of the MTTB leaders in the thirties and who was now Minister of Education. One of the aims of the society appears to have been to infiltrate the educational system, and it attempted to gain control of TMTF, succeeding to the extent that it temporarily captured some of the subsidiary organs. TMTF's struggles against reaction in general and against the Türk Milliyetciler Derneği and İleri specifically brought the organization into sharp conflict with the government; Prime Minister Menderes denied that there was a wave of reaction and accused TMTF several times of involvement in politics. Finally, the students won their campaign thanks, rather surprisingly, to the intervention of President Bayar, whose attitude on this issue apparently differed from that of Menderes. At a meeting in 1953, TMTF leaders allayed Bayar's suspicions that they had ties to the CHP, that their actions were at all politically motivated, and produced evidence showing that İleri was packing the Ministry of Education with his sympathizers. A month later, İleri, another minister, and two deputies were expelled from the DP (they were later readmitted). From then on, Bayar was favorably disposed to TMTF and sponsored an annual ball in its behalf to provide the organization with an independent source of income. His one condition was that TMTF not engage in politics.

Such a demand reflected the DP view of student politicization, a view that, like the one held by the CHP, was motivated at least partly by political considerations. After it came to power, the DP sought to keep the students out of the political arena, and Prime Minister Menderes frequently condemned the involvement of students in political issues. Prior to 1950, however, when it was clear that the mass of the students was supporting the DP, the leaders of that party remained silent and it was İsmet İnönü who, in his Taksim speech, spoke out against student politicization. By 1953, however, it was the turn of the CHP leaders to ignore the issue, for they possessed close links with the students.

Essentially, both parties were concerned with the political power and influence of students and their organizations. The transition toward a multiparty system and the accompanying relaxation of repressive controls had allowed MTTB and TMTF to establish themselves firmly, and the struggle for power within the political arena led inexorably to the development of close linkages between students and political actors and growing student involvement in political affairs. Their politicization was, in fact, an ironic tribute to the important position they achieved within Turkish society, and to the high regard in which they were held by practicing politicians of all parties who viewed both MTTB and TMTF as extremely useful instruments for propaganda, agitation, and pressure, and as important resources available to a party for creating issues, arousing public opinion, and organizing demonstrations.

Thus, leaders of all parties viewed the student organizations in terms of their own position within the polity and followed policies that were often contrary to student interests. The most obvious example involves the many attempts to merge the two student organizations, dating back to the early fifties, all of which ended in failure. This was partly due to the fears of MTTB leaders that they would be swallowed up by the stronger TMTF and that their chances for office would disappear, and partly to the composition of MTTB, in which students from technical institutes who were not eligible for TMTF membership predominated, but in a greater degree to the reluctance of the political parties to see one organization established. In 1953, for example, MTTB signed a convention on unity with TMTF, but the MTTB Congress rejected it amid widespread charges in the press that Suphi Baykam, who chaired the sessions, had been ordered by the CHP to ensure that the two organizations would not merge (Yeni Sabah, 1953). Tevfik İleri once told some student leaders very bluntly why he and other political leaders were opposed to unity: "It is not in my interest politically. If there are two organizations and one is opposed to me I can get control of the other and public opinion doesn't really know which is which."

As the 1954 elections approached, however, the government decided to change its policy toward the student organizations. Concerned with its diminishing legitimacy among intellectuals and students, it moved to maintain a posture of friendliness toward TMTF but to capture control of MTTB. Two explanations have been suggested for this dual policy; first, it apparently felt that TMTF was not as hostile as MTTB, perhaps due to Bayar's influence; and second, since MTTB was the weaker organization and possessed a unitary structure, whereas TMTF was a solidly based federation, it was much easier to gain control of the former.

To oust the pro-CHP faction that was in control of MTTB, however, did not prove a simple matter, and only after a bitter struggle was a pro-government student elected president of MTTB. Both the previous

[40]

state of MTTB/government relations and the consequences of the election are indicated by the following comment from his first annual report (MTTB, 1953):

> As a result of the conclusion that the bad atmosphere which was created in the eyes of the government against our organization was due to the lack of close relations with the government, this year we established close contacts.

Following his period in office and the completion of his military obligation, he formally joined the DP.

TMTF, on the other hand, enjoyed close and continuing contacts with the government, and received a considerable amount of support from it. The following list of visits made in the first six months of 1953 and the issues that were discussed (TMTF, 1954) indicates the degree of access to the highest government leaders that TMTF enjoyed, as well as the kinds of assistance that it requested. Meetings were held with President Bayar twice (to discuss the ball and other problems); with Refik Koraltan, Speaker of the Grand National Assembly (financial assistance); with the Minister of Education four times (student problems); the Minister of Foreign Affairs (Cyprus and visits of foreign students); ministers of state three times (student problems, financial assistance); the Minister of Finance (financial assistance); the Minister of Agriculture (transportation for village trips); the Minister of Customs and Monopolies (duty-free liquor and tobacco for the ball); the Minister of Communications (financial assistance for a planned celebration of the five hundredth anniversary of the capture of Istanbul); the Minister of Press and Tourism (tourism problems); the Istanbul and Ankara valis and mayors several times each (financial assistance, student problems).

Nevertheless, despite such close ties, friction between the government and student leaders continued because the organizations were not passive monolithic institutions, but possessed an ethos and personality of their own, and much depended upon the delicate interplay of personalities within any organization. Thus, although one particular group might gain control, to maintain itself in power was often no easy matter, and the resulting interplay within the organization often led to the adoption of positions on issues that did not conform to the government's official line. One notable example involved MTTB after the DP had elected one of its members as president in 1953. Despite the continuing insistence by the government that there was no reaction within the country, MTTB continued its stand on this issue, and its leaders signed pronouncements that were embarrassing to the government. They apparently felt the need to cooperate with TMTF on this matter, partly because of genuine differences of opinion on this issue within their own ranks, but also because the MTTB president felt it advisable to conform to the prevailing mood of the students within and outside the organization.

The DP's sensitivity to student activism became particularly apparent after 1954. In that year, it won an overwhelming victory at the polls, for its program of economic development had led to a marked increase in rural well-being. Encouraged by this evidence of popular support, the government accelerated its ambitious program of economic and social change, but haphazard planning, adverse terms of trade, large defense expenditures, and a shortage of capital resulted not in growth, but in a drastic inflation, scarcity of consumer items, and increased tension within the polity. Affected most by this economic crisis were the urban elements, especially intellectuals, bureaucrats, and military officers whose status within the society continued to drop as social standing became ever more correlated with wealth. Not surprisingly, criticism and opposition grew within the country—the first efforts by military officers to organize a revolution date back to 1954—and the national political climate deteriorated rapidly as the government proved intolerant of opposition and adopted various restrictive measures to limit the rights of free speech, assembly, campaigning, and the autonomy of the universities. These moves only accelerated the alienation of all intellectuals and other "modern" segments of the society, including students, from the government which, in turn, became even more repressive and amended the electoral laws to strengthen its position. Thus, though the DP was again successful at the polls in 1957, the results served to increase ill-will between various segments of the society reflected in the growing bitterness between the two major parties. In short, as the government's legitimacy dropped, it increased repression within the society with important consequences for the student movement and political developments in general.

In this environment, the students developed increased political consciousness, and their concerns underwent a marked change. Now they became increasingly concerned with questions of freedom and democracy and, in 1956, for the first time, a student protest erupted that did not involve either communism or reaction. The setting was the Political Science Faculty of Ankara University, which, in government eyes, had become a stronghold of the CHP. In December of that year, the popular Dean, Turhan Feyzioğlu, was dismissed by the government on the charge of having engaged in political activity. Actually, he had denounced the government's refusal to promote a colleague who had criticized official policies. Three hundred students boycotted classes in protest and 221 signed a telegram to President Celâl Bayar (Taylak, 1969: 238 ff.).

The incident marked a watershed in student-government relations. The government's legitimacy dropped even further in the eyes of the university community and, as the domestic political climate became increasingly acrimonious, TMTF began to take stronger and more open positions on domestic issues. Although TMTF never adopted a pro-CHP policy, the stands that it took were critical of the government and, hence, helpful to the opposition. Thus TMTF became identified, more and more in DP eyes, as a tool of the CHP, particularly when a student who was active in that party and head of its provincial youth organization was elected president.

The government decided to react as it had earlier when MTTB was supportive of the opposition, and it moved to subvert TMTF. To do so, however, proved no easy or cheap matter because of the organization's structure and strength, and a huge sum—600,000 TL—reportedly was spent to elect a DP loyalist as president.

This expensive success proved illusory, as the government's legitimacy dropped even further in student eyes, and their mood turned ever more strongly against the administration. Thus, although MTTB was in the hands of DP supporters, the inner feuding was such that no congress was held for three years. When one was finally convened in 1959, 30,000 TL were reportedly spent to ensure that the next president was also friendly toward the DP. Nevertheless, as the political atmosphere continued to deteriorate, both MTTB and TMTF refused to take pro-DP positions, a further indication of the autonomous aspects of student organizations that we have already noted. In 1960, the two presidents declared, "We are neither CHP nor DP nor CKMP"; subsequently the DP ceased its financial support to MTTB (Taylak, 1969: 274-278). These actions took place in a rapidly deteriorating political atmosphere as the first three months of 1960 witnessed a series of incidents that suggested that the government wanted to kill İsmet İnönü and destroy all opposition. A special commission was established to investigate the CHP, and the decision to grant it extraordinary powers seemed to herald a further steep increase in repression. The result was not a dictatorship, but student demonstrations which triggered the revolution of May 27, 1960.

While these developments were occurring within the polity and the student organizations, higher education in Turkey was undergoing a considerable amount of change; change that also affected the student activism we have discussed. In two important respects, the changes in the political system were paralleled by developments in higher education. Both deteriorated during the fifties, and both became subject to far less government control than had been the case heretofore.

As part of the liberalization that followed World War II, the Universities Law of 1946 granted practically total autonomy to the universities. The management of university affairs was entrusted to academic bodies and the universities were organized around independent faculties which consisted, as in Germany, of a number of "chairs" in specific subjects. Unfortunately, the chair system and the process by which a person became a faculty member and advanced up the academic ladder proved to be extremely rigid and concentrated power in the hands of a few individuals within the faculties, so that personal considerations came to dominate almost all aspects of university life, to the obvious detriment of scholarly activity. Nor could the many abuses that developed be controlled by the administrative machinery since power and responsibility were now vested within the individual faculties. Hence, before long, the universities were facing serious problems of morale, discipline, and intellectual rigor with important consequences for student unrest.

These weaknesses were greatly aggravated by the explosion in enrollments which took place during this period, particularly in the lycées, whose number rose from 83 in 1945 to 194 in 1960, the number of graduates, practically all of whom sought to continue their education, jumping from 25,515 to 75,632. The government was unwilling to withstand these pressures, and the total number of students receiving a higher education exploded from 20,000 in 1945 to over 53,000 in 1960. Particularly affected were the nonscientific fields—the percentage of students enrolled in the social sciences increased from 44% in 1949 to 50% in 1959, whereas the percentage of those enrolled in scientific and technological fields actually declined from 44% to 40% of the total— though the absolute number did increase (Organization for Economic Cooperation and Development, 1965: 82).

The government's concern with expansion did not extend to the provision of adequate inputs of physical and human resources, and the increase in teaching staffs lagged far behind enrollments, particularly in the social sciences. Thus, though the number of professors in this field rose from 199 to 484 during this period, the student-teacher ratio deteriorated from 1:37 to 1:50. In the arts and sciences, it dropped from 1:14 to 1:18; in the fine arts, from 1:1 to 1:3; and in higher agricultural education, from 1:7 to 1:10. In higher technical education and in health education, it improved from 1:9 to 1:6 and from 1:15 to 1:6, respectively (Organization for Economic Cooperation and Development, 1965: 155-156).

The shortage of faculty was aggravated by the fact that many of the available staff members devoted a considerable amount of time to positions outside the university, despite a legal limitation on the time that could be devoted to such occupations. They did so both because of economic pressures—salaries of professors remained unchanged during the inflation which characterized Turkey from 1955 onward—but also because many persons entered the academic world solely in order to gain the prestige that would enable them to pursue a lucrative professional career.

Thus, many faculty would visit the university for a few hours each week to deliver a lecture to a mass of students. Such traditional teaching methods remained the norm, and little interaction ever took place between students and faculty. Seldom was there any opportunity for discussion or for questions to be asked of the professor during his lecture and student-faculty contacts outside the classroom were severely limited. Even if a faculty member had the inclination to meet with students, the sheer numbers made it difficult for any genuine relationships to develop.

Reinforcing this impersonal climate was the traditional emphasis upon rote learning. The goal of every student was essentially to memorize enough of the faculty member's book or his lecture notes, which were readily available, to pass the examinations, the only basis of success or failure. Three months of the nine-month academic year were devoted to these examinations, often oral, in which the student was expected to demonstrate that he had memorized a certain set of facts. Under these considerations, even serious students possessed little incentive to attend classes or to study at any time except prior to examinations. Many students chose not to study even then, since there was no requirement that they take final examinations, and they were free to repeat a course as often as they wished.

The serious shortage of such physical facilities as classrooms and libraries also served to discourage serious academic work on the part of many. Despite the growth in law school enrollments, for example, from 4,217 in 1945 to 14,531 in 1960, the largest auditorium at Ankara and Istanbul universities holds only a few hundred persons, thus making it impossible for the majority of students to attend any given lecture (Redden, 1957: 42). A similar situation existed with regard to library facilities. Here, too, facilities were inadequate both in terms of the number of books, their accessibility, the training of librarians, and the physical plant. To give but one illustration, the library of Istanbul University was housed in a building which had been declared unsafe. Only members of the academic staff could check books out, though senior students were allowed to make use of its facilities. In most libraries, subject indexes were lacking, and filing was by date of acquisition, thus making it very difficult for even the most dedicated researcher to locate needed materials.

In addition to problems of physical facilities, teaching staffs, and methods of instruction, two other factors served to lower the quality of the universities during this period. First, the expansion of educational opportunities at the secondary level had similar unfortunate consequences for the standard of lycée instruction which, in many schools, particularly the newer ones in remote areas, was of very low quality. Thus, the universities found that many students arrived ill-prepared for college work (Sarç, 1966: 113-114; Okyar, 1968).

Second, the great demand for a university education was not always motivated by the desire of a student to obtain a degree. Many persons enrolled in whatever faculty happened to have space available, regardless of the subject, in order to avoid military service or to qualify for the many benefits which a university student received. These included a 25% discount for admission to movies, theatre, or opera; a discount of from 33.33 to 75 percent for local transportation, and a 50 percent reduction for all rail and sea travel within Turkey (Redden, 1957: 44). Supplementing these financial benefits was the high prestige accorded to a university student, and many youths, especially from Anatolia, who were eager to gain this status in the eyes of their families, friends, and acquaintances, succeeded in entering the universities.

Under these conditions, it is not surprising that academic standards deteriorated rapidly after World War II. The percentage of students graduated in four or five years dropped precipitously in this period. It was estimated, for example, that, in 1946, 26 percent of the students enrolled in the Law School at Istanbul University successfully completed their course of study within five years, but by 1958 the number stood at 8 percent. The situation was even worse in the Faculty of Letters. There it was estimated that, between 1950 and 1958, only 15 percent of the freshmen ever became sophomores and that only 6 percent of these graduated within five years (Mediko-Sosyal Merkezi, 1965: 12). Even the elite Political Science Faculty suffered, the percentage of students there who passed without delay dropped from over 75 percent in 1955 to less than half in 1964 (Abadan, 1965: 72). Thus, being a university student became more than ever a frustrating experience. Only a very small number were serious and successful students, and even fewer ever had the opportunity to appreciate the true meaning of higher education or to develop an interest in genuine intellectual achievement. For the majority, being a student came to represent a way of life that had little relationship to the pursuit of knowledge, and, as conditions within the universities deteriorated, so the malaise among the students became more and more deep-rooted, and feelings of resentment and alienation became more and more prevalent.

The deteriorating economic and social conditions of student life also served to reinforce the general feeling of discontent and frustration generated by the academic environment. Very few students worked their way through college—only 1½ percent of the Istanbul University students have jobs—(Mediko-Sosyal Merkezi, 1965: 11), and only a small number of very inadequate fellowships were available—6 percent of the students received fellowship assistance of some kind (TMTF, n.d.: 8). The great majority were totally dependent upon their families for their income, and, as a result of the inflation, many families found themselves unable to provide their children with an adequate allowance. The standard of living of most students, never high, dropped sharply; according to one estimate, the average student income was about 200-250 TL per month, a figure which did not permit the enjoyment of many luxuries (TMTF, n.d.: 7).[8]

Most of the students' income had to be spent for lodging and meals, and the number of dormitories, canteens, and cafeterias, inadequate for many years, never expanded to meet the needs of growing enrollments. In 1962, dormitory space was available to only 12,104 students. More facilities were available in Ankara than in Istanbul, where only 17 percent of the students were living in dormitories, and 33 percent were renting quarters. In Ankara, on the other hand, 38 percent were living in dormitories and only 8 percent were living in rented quarters. The remainder lived at home, 32 percent and 47 percent, respectively; or with relatives, 9 percent and 6 percent (Mediko-Sosyal Merkezi, 1965: 13; Ozankaya, 1966: 24). The fundamental reason for this state of affairs lay in political considerations. For years there has been talk, in Istanbul, of a university city with adequate facilities, but many cynical students have suggested that the main reason why this plan has never materialized is the fear by all governments of a large concentration of students in one location.

The organization of the dormitories also had important consequences for the functioning of the student organizations. Dormitories are classified according to region, so that all the students from a province are assigned to the same one. Most of these students already know each other very well since they graduated from the same lycées, but the dormitory arrangement serves to reinforce these existing ties and to make regionalism an important factor in accounting for the leadership which emerged within the student organizations. In the fifties, many of the student leaders came from the Eastern provinces, but in the early sixties students from the Black Sea coast won positions of prominence, especially within TMTF.

Election to student office, however, entails not only the solid support of a dormitory, but alliances with representatives from other regions and the support of the delegates who will be attending the congress at which officers will be elected. A successful campaign thus necessitated time, money, and organization. It was estimated that about a year of strenuous effort was required to win election as president of TMTF, and, as the organization became increasingly active and politicized, fewer and fewer genuine students were willing to devote this length of time to campaigning or possessed the necessary contacts to obtain financing and support. Thus, as we have noted, political activists gained control first of MTTB, and later of TMTF, with significant consequences for their development and, indeed, for the country's political struggle.

Nor were conditions in the dormitories particularly attractive—four to eight students usually shared one room—and most students preferred to spend as little time as possible in their quarters. Since recreational facilities were meager, favorite student pastimes included sitting in coffeehouses, strolling aimlessly with friends, and going to the movies—usually more than once a week. One study has noted that this heavy movie attendance, by providing dream substitutes grounded in Western frames of reference, tends to heighten the already pronounced emotional instability which characterizes many students, who are faced with tormenting psychological problems caused by their emancipation from parental control and their new-found freedom. Essentially, they are confronted with a conflict between tradition and modernity, and serious tensions often result. Perhaps the overriding issue making for frustration is that of male-female relationships, for it is in this area that traditional social mores conflict most strongly with the pattern of behavior portrayed in foreign movies and with the realities of university life (Abadan, 1963: 84, 1961: 63 ff.). The psychological dissonance generated by these conflicts is enhanced by such exposure to conditions in more affluent societies so that the tendency toward frustration and alienation among the students which was generated by their educational, social, and economic environment was greatly increased.

Such feelings were shared by most students who, despite the unprecedented expansion of the Turkish educational system at all levels, were still largely of middle- and upper-class urban backgrounds. The degree to which educational opportunities remained restricted has been summarized (Kazamias, 1966: 171) as follows:

(a) Of 100 primary school students, about 13 can expect to enter a middle-level institution; less than 3 can expect to enter a lycée, about 1 can expect to enter a university.

(b) Of 100 middle school students, about 26 can expect to enter a lycée; about 14 can expect to enter a university.

(c) Of 100 lycée students, about 55 can expect to enter a university; about 86, an institution of higher learning.

The lower and upper secondary levels represented the two major bottlenecks, and at both these stages the urban child benefits greatly from the concentration of middle schools and lycées in towns and cities. Furthermore, there was a vast discrepancy in the quality of different lycées, and students who graduated from those located in Ankara and Istanbul, especially the private ones, stood the best chance of gaining admission to the faculty of their choice. Thus the faculties with the greatest prestige, such as the Political Science Faculty, secured the best-prepared students, largely children of educated, well-to-do urban dwellers.

This is reflected in the available data for this period which, though limited, somewhat contradictory, and subject to varying margins of error, show that from 34 to 54 percent of the students at Ankara University were children of bureaucrats and army officers, and from 6-14 percent were the children of professionals. Seventy percent of those enrolled in the Political Science Faculty possessed a similar background. In Istanbul University, 29 percent of the students were children of bureaucrats and army officers; 18 percent, of professionals. The remainder were primarily children of businessmen, merchants, and landowners (see Appendix). This was particularly true of girls who tended to come from the most advanced strata of society as measured by parental education and occupation. Eighty percent of the Ankara girl students were daughters of professionals, officers, or bureaucrats, and 47 percent of their fathers and 6 percent of their mothers were university graduates (Ozankaya, 1966: 100-101).

It was precisely these groups who were most affected by the consequences of the DP policies. Not only were they opposed on ideological grounds, but the income of all on fixed salaries—especially government officials, army officers, and many intellectuals—declined greatly owing to the inflation. At the same time, social status became more closely correlated with economic power, so that new groups in Turkish society were gaining positions of power and influence at their expense. That these developments should have reinforced the anti-government stance of the students who regarded the DP as endangering the economic development of the country, its democratization, and the Ataturk reforms, is not surprising. Furthermore, many of the students were aiming for careers in the civil service, and they could see the prestige and financial rewards attached to such positions decline rapidly, while competition for the available posts was increasing as enrollments in the faculties swelled.

Thus, by 1960, students were suffering from strong feelings of relative deprivation occasioned by their worsening economic and academic environment, gloomy perceptions of future opportunities, and serious concern with the shape of political events. The expectations of the early fifties had been rudely dashed, and it now appeared that not only was the country not modernizing, but the principles of the Ataturk revolution itself were in serious danger. Complementing the linkage of relative deprivation between the student subsystem and the polity were the strong ties that we have emphasized between students and various political actors. Given the strength of these linkages and the character of the political system, low regime legitimacy, and medium repressiveness (that now appeared to be rising drastically), it is not surprising that students precipitated the revolution of May 27.

There seems little doubt that the CHP welcomed the politicization of the students and their opposition to the government and its policies and encouraged this trend in various ways so as to increase tensions within the polity. On the anniversary of his famous victory during the War of Independence, for example, 1,000 university students visited former president İnönü and joined the CHP. On that occasion, he declared, "In the coming days important duties will be awaiting you. You will be victorious. We trust the youth" (Taylak, 1969: 274). Moreover, the CHP's youth organization was involved in the demonstration that erupted at Istanbul University on April 28. The night before, students went from dormitory to dormitory to announce that a meeting would be held the following morning (İpekci and Coşar, 1965: 139) to protest the expulsion of İnönü from the Assembly for his strong stand against the law which gave the government's investigating committee extensive dictatorial powers. In the morning, students gathered around Ataturk's statue and when, despite the rector's opposition, police entered the inviolate university grounds, violence soon erupted in which over 10,000 students were eventually involved.

The news of the rioting spread rapidly, and the following day about

4,000 students from the Ankara Political Science Faculty and the Law Faculty protested the events which had taken place in Istanbul. One student who participated in the Ankara demonstration has described them as follows:

> I saw all the students in the lobby. . . . We joined with the students of the neighboring law school. . . . We sang our national anthem. . . . We yelled against Menderes. . . . We loved freedom and decided to fight for it. The police and the soldiers surrounded both schools. . . . The commander ordered us to disappear but nobody listened. The police attacked the students of the law school and chased them until the students entered their classrooms. Some of the students were wounded. . . . We hated the policemen and . . . prepared barricades behind all the doors; we made piles of stones. We threw stones at the police. . . . The soldiers . . . fired upon us. We escaped inside the building. They shot at the building and the windows. . . . All the policemen were inside now. They were shooting everywhere. They made us prisoners inside a room. . . . A few minutes later some of the army officers came in and threw the policemen out. They told us to go to our classes. We discussed the matter with our professors who were very excited too. . . . The officers told us that we were free and we could go to our homes [Göhalp, 1961: 7,9].

Faculty members were heavily involved in all these events and it would be a mistake to underestimate the role of faculty in student activism. At Istanbul University, one professor delivered, on the morning of April 28, a fiery lecture on liberty and freedom to his class on constitutional law. The same day "some of the Political Science Faculty professors also didn't want to give the lessons and talked about human rights—against the government. I was sure that our fight would be even more bloody in Ankara than it had been in Istanbul." On April 29, "The teachers didn't come to the classes either but encouraged the students." Some participated actively in the riots and "took a leading part in resisting the police" (Göhalp, 1961: 7, 9; London Times, 1960; Weiker, 1963: 15 ff.).

In an attempt to ease the tension, the government closed the universities for a month, thus allowing the students to go home and spread news of the situation throughout the country. Sporadic demonstrations by students continued throughout May, mainly in Ankara, but the outbreaks of April 28-29 proved to be the decisive event that triggered the army into action on May 27.

FROM REVOLUTION TO INTERVENTION

The revolution of 1960 had an exhilarating effect upon students and intellectuals, but it proved no simple matter to deal with the many serious problems confronting the country. The military junta found itself forced to remain in power for almost eighteen months while it sought to resolve the conditions which led to the uprising, to deal with the arrested DP leaders, and to legitimize the military takeover because the country remained divided along essentially the same lines as in the late fifties. On one side were the groups who had supported the DP and who now voted for its successor, the AP (Justice Party); on the the other, those who had welcomed the revolution.

To rebuild a political consensus under these conditions was no easy matter. A series of weak coalition governments which proved incapable of resolving the major problems dividing the society ruled the country under the watchful eye of the military, and two attempted coups had to be suppressed. Thus, the first half of the sixties was characterized by intense competition between various political groupings and parties for political advantage, and the polity could be considered as possessing low legitimacy in the eyes of most students and intellectuals. As we shall see later, this competition was reflected in the character of the student movement itself. The 1965 elections did not alter the situation greatly. Despite the CHP's attempt to portray itself as a left-of-center party dedicated to reform, the AP, under the leadership of Suleyman Demirel, swept to a decisive victory. For several years, Mr. Demirel was able to maintain the unity of the liberal and conservative wings of his party, and to retain the confidence of the military. The country enjoyed a remarkable degree of freedom and a quite rapid rate of economic growth, though it was accompanied by many problems including a chronic inflation. Despite these considerable achievements, however, many important issues such as land reform, tax reform, and educational reform that intellectuals regarded as crucial for the future welfare of the society, were never undertaken. Moreover, the sixties witnessed the fragmentation of several parties, either formally or informally, and political tensions were exacerbated by the ensuing conflicts within and among these groupings. Thus, the country remained divided, and most students and intellectuals were increasingly alienated from a political system that was characterized by inadequate policy outputs and that did not hold the promise of consolidation and development. The result was low legitimacy accompanied by low repression, conditions that were to deeply affect the student movement.[9]

Essentially, the trends of the late fifties were now aggravated and accelerated, and this decade witnessed a remarkable shift in the tone, style, and frequency of student activism. Now that there was increasing resort to violent action, meetings, and manifestos, campaigns on national and international issues became almost daily events, as did physical confrontations between various student factions. Even the student declarations reflected their growing militancy. According to one study (Abadan, 1963: 90), those issued before May 27, 1960, were:

> more of an indicative nature, carrying only the purpose to inform public opinion whereas the nature of those published after the revolution are much more dynamic, requesting quick action, containing warnings and sometimes even threats.

Accompanying these changes was a shift in the political affiliation of many students. In the new, liberalized atmosphere that followed the revolution, leftist ideas and publications which had heretofore been suppressed were widely distributed, and a pronounced trend to the left became evident. Contributing greatly to this development were the efforts of a new Marxist party (TIP). Soon after its inception in 1961, a young lawyer, M. Ali Aybar, was elected to its presidency, reorganized the party, and launched an energetic campaign to gain support among students. Before long, it had won a large following in the universities, as increasing numbers of students and intellectuals turned to socialism as an ideology which provided a solution to the serious social and economic problems confronting Turkey.

Thus, a drastic shift in the ideological orientation of the students is discernible after 1960. From 1946 to 1960, they were preoccupied with three major issues: anti-communism, which declined rapidly in importance; the protection of the Ataturk reforms and the fight against reaction; and the Cyprus question. In the sixties, however, students became most concerned with questions of social justice and economic development and were deeply affected by events within the international system, including student activism elsewhere. While Cyprus remained an important factor, students now gave primary attention to domestic and international problems, and words like imperialism, reaction, Vietnam, socialism, and social justice became commonplace. These words reflect the ideological orientations of the majority of students who, by the mid-sixties, could be classified as leftists of one sort or another, although important ideological differences could be discerned among them. The essential pattern, however, was one of opposition to existing social, economic, and political institutions, and hence of violent anti-Americanism, since the United States was regarded as an imperial power supporting the reactionary AP government through such channels as NATO. The legitimacy of the political system was lowest among the most active students. One study conducted in 1964-1965 indicated that they were far less interested in Cyprus and far more concerned with domestic problems on which they adopted more extreme positions than most students. Moreover, whereas only 6 percent of the students stated they would vote for TIP and 48 percent supported the CHP, 25 percent of the activists said they preferred TIP, 36 percent the CHP (Ozankaya, 1966: 75).

The apparent support accorded to the CHP by students was deceptive, for increasing numbers lost faith in the party in this period. Discontent with the weakness and ineffectiveness of the coalition governments which it headed became widespread, and there was a growing feeling that the party was moribund and could not provide the country with strong leadership. The weakness of the CHP was an important factor prompting İnönü's decision, on the eve of the 1965 elections, to project the CHP as a left-of-center party modelled after the social democratic parties of Western Europe. This ideological change, however, did not suffice to revitalize the party, and it did not do well in the election. Nor did the shift halt the steady erosion of student and intellectual support toward TIP, and, by the late sixties, the CHP enjoyed only a small part of the overwhelming support it had possessed among these groups prior to 1960. How drastic a shift actually took place is indicated by the way in which students in 18 dormitories in Ankara, Istanbul, and Izmir voted in 1961 and 1965. In the former election, the CHP received 64 percent of the student vote; in 1965, only 32 percent voted for the CHP and 47 percent for TIP (Genç, 1971: 24). Many students actively worked in behalf of TIP as well. Before the 1965 elections, the student organization of the METU spent 35,000 TL organizing for TIP in 46 districts (Genç, 1971: 24).

This change, however, did not alter the character of the basic polarization within the country, though it served to increase the bitterness and tension associated with it. The AP, which had emerged as the heir of the DP and the strongest party in the country, was practically as unpopular among the students and intellectuals as the DP had been before the 1960 revolution. In October 1962, and again in March 1963, students staged major demonstrations directed against that party and its policies. Thus, the foundations for a repetition of past events were laid as the government once again came to regard the student opposition as a threat that had to be controlled. Its opponents, on the other hand, regarded the students as important political tools to be used to strengthen their own position. In this atmosphere of high politicization, many aspects of the fifties were once again evident and many of the same events, though now in a highly aggravated fashion, were to occur.

As before, an early casualty was student unity. After the revolution, responsible student leaders had hoped that the traditional division between TMTF and MTTB could now be ended and a revitalized organization that genuinely represented student interests created. Such a goal, however, simply could not be achieved under existing political conditions. Thus, though TMTF and MTTB signed a protocol in 1962 which provided for a single organization, it was never implemented. Why this was so was openly expressed by the president of TMTF (1963) in a press conference designed to speed action when he stated:

> The existence of two organizations has always been an obstacle to the solving of the problems of Turkish college youth. . . . If the politicians genuinely want MTTB and TMTF to unite and if they do not possess a low thought like wishing to have a tool for political purposes they will pass a law.

Shortly after the ensuing publicity, the Minister of Education met with representatives of MTTB and TMTF who agreed to prepare a draft law which they submitted to him on July 6, 1963. No further action was ever taken.

Not only was unity not to be achieved, but the government decided to take steps to ease the pressure generated by the students and to counterbalance the successful efforts of TIP to mobilize students in its behalf. Once again, and for the same reasons, the decision was made to gain control of MTTB, and a lengthy, bitter, and well-publicized struggle between "leftists" and "rightists" ensued within the organization. The latter faction finally emerged victorious in an irregular congress held in Bursa in 1965 after, according to one student, an investment by the government of 24,500 TL (Genç, 1971: 27). Perhaps as a reward for his success, the student who was elected president later became an AP deputy (Genç, 1971: 28). The reactionary stance that MTTB now assumed is reflected in a statement by one of its leaders, who declared in 1968: "İnönü was the one who opened the way to Western culture and communism in Turkey . . . if it had not been for the Islamic religion the whole country would have turned red" (Genç, 1971: 87). The following year, the AP decided to extend its influence over TMTF as well, and once again a bitter struggle ensued, though this time the pro-government delegates were defeated. Nevertheless, the losers held their own congress and those elected were hailed by the government press as the true leaders of TMTF (Genç, 1971: 41-45).

By the mid-sixties, such practices had become extremely common. In fact, the ways in which power was obtained and maintained within a student association would have done credit to any corrupt city machine in the United States, and charges of fraud, corruption, and trickery were commonly exchanged by rival factions. In 1965, for example, one group attempting to gain control of the Istanbul University Student Association, a subsidiary organ of TMTF, accused the incumbent president in a six-page communique of violating the bylaws, misusing funds, favoring hometown friends, packing a congress, and various irresponsible and illegal behavior of all sorts (IUTB, n.d.). In many cases, such charges were manufactured; in others, one faction would resort to physical force to seize headquarters in order to obtain documents and records which could be used to expose the corrupt practices of the incumbents. Fraudulent devices of all kinds were also utilized in order to gain control of and to hold on to office. Elections were often a farce, being held in taxis or even washrooms by three or four persons, and the phrase "kidnapped congress" entered the language.

As such practices once again became commonplace, the character and type of student leadership was transformed, and professionals emerged in positions of control. Such a shift may have been inevitable given the considerable amount of time required to achieve office and maintain oneself in power. It was not possible to be a full-time, serious student and simultaneously occupy a key office within a student organization as evidenced by the experience of a TMTF president in the early sixties, before the union became heavily politicized, who served a one-year term. Though his only concern was to administer its many activities efficiently, he still found it impossible to devote much time to academic pursuits and fell a full year behind in his studies. His successor, a professional student, had been enrolled at Istanbul University for seven years before finally becoming a sophomore in the law school in 1965. How common this problem was is indicated by the report of a European expert who surveyed the Turkish student movement in these years and concluded (Devrim Gençliği, 1965: 8): "I learned with great sorrow that a great many of the most successful administrators have not yet graduated. They cannot pursue their studies successfully while working for TMTF; TMTF damaged their studies."

Many persons were, of course, perfectly willing to spend their time in running a student association, for such tenure still represented an important investment in one's future. Student leaders remained national figures with ready access to leading personalities in and out of government, and many regarded leadership positions in the student organizations as a means of gaining important contacts and a knowledge of skills and techniques in administration, public speaking, and politics which could later be translated into prestigious and remunerative positions either in a professional career or, more commonly, with a political party. Such a background was especially desirable for an aspiring politician, since one of the factors making for power and prestige within a party was the ability to claim a large student following. Moreover, large financial sums were involved. In the sixties, millions of lira were paid by the state to student organizations without any attempt to check on the actual disbursement of the funds (Genç, 1971: 16). Supplementing these resources were the sizeable inputs that were made by political parties, directly or indirectly, as they sought ways to establish and maintain control over the students. The city of Istanbul's council, for example, which was controlled by the AP, allocated 80,000 TL to MTTB in 1967 alone (Genç, 1971: 76).

The ties between student activists and political actors became so close and intense during these years that not only were close links between parties and specific student groupings within an association established, but often different factions within a single party sought to influence developments within a student union for its own advantage in the party's internal struggle. Since the AP, the CHP, and the TIP were all split internally, the result was the further splintering of the student associations into factional disarray. The degree to which this was indeed the case and what this meant in practice for the functioning of the associations was vividly illustrated by the disclosure in the press of a letter written by one student to a CHP leader who was fighting for control of the party:[10]

> I do my best that our position in the party requires. It is regrettable that people who had no function in the party up to recent times have now become top personalities in the party because of chance and events in closed rooms. I think that it will be necessary to get control of MTTB again in the future. As our country is lying on the operation table, this point is very important and very necessary for the future position of our group in the party. . . . I think that I can convince the persons who are considered to be against us. If this cannot be done I can label them . . . as enemies of Ataturk and the Reforms and so I can drive them out. Because of my activities and in order to prevent the dispersal of our supporters, I am requesting some financial assistance. If I were not in financial difficulties. . . . I

would not bother you. I hope that you will appreciate my situation and I express my belief that you will do that which is necessary [Yeni İstanbul, 1965].

Thus, within the associations, it soon became possible to identify ideological shadings that corresponded more or less closely to the characteristics of practically every political grouping within the country. Most important in this regard were the divisions within TIP, as we shall see below.

Politicization and corruption reached such levels in these years that even the umbrella youth organization, *Türkiye Milli Gençlik Teşkilati*, felt the need to publicly endorse legislation to eliminate prevailing abuses. A strong editorial in its magazine called for a thorough reform of the student associations and pointed out that in many instances the organizations were "under the monopoly of . . . professionals . . . who have exerted no effort other than to obtain financial benefits for themselves" and who "used the associations as a tool for their own political, ideological and doctrinal opinions." It especially criticized existing electoral practices, noting that the overriding concern of the activists was to gain office and to retain power using whatever means were necessary, and specifically mentioned frequent instances of an officer refusing to convene a scheduled meeting, or adjourning one already in session, when the outcome of an election was in doubt. It noted that, in such an environment, although "congresses continue for several days and tens of thousands of liras are spent, no student problem is seriously discussed," and that the atmosphere is usually not that of a "conflict of ideas . . . but almost like a street fight." It concluded that these practices "have almost frightened . . . eligible, honest, and normal students from even participating in the organizations" (Gençlik, 1965: 10-11).

The decline in the standing of MTTB and TMTF among students started in the 1950s when both unions were stuffed with party activists trying to gain control and support and secret police trying to keep track of developments for the government. Before long, the more serious students became almost totally disillusioned and, by 1961, it was estimated that 50 percent of the students did not consider TMTF or MTTB to be an important part of university life, and 20 percent thought they were unnecessary (Abadan, 1961: 76-77). Subsequently, these percentages rose even higher; it was estimated in the late sixties that less than half the students took an interest in the organizations' activities, and only about 10% of this group, primarily students with political ambitions and militants, were really active. A study conducted at Ankara University showed that only 22 percent of the students were members of any club and that the officers tended to be upperclassmen, somewhat older than the other students, had fathers who were bureaucrats or army officers, and, in general, had parents who were better educated and possessed a higher income than the other students (Ozankaya, 1966: 77, 20-21).

Moreover, the student unions simultaneously lost their standing with the general public. The widespread publicity that their practices and conditions received severely damaged their reputation and, consequently, their effectiveness. No longer were they regarded by the educated urban elite as idealistic youth dedicated to the maintenance of the Ataturk ideals, but rather as decadent organizations manipulated by politicians for selfish reasons and run by professional students who were corrupt or anxious to make a political career for themselves or by militants seeking to destroy the system.

Discontent with the student subsystem was not limited to this dimension alone, for while these events were occurring, the academic environment also continued to deteriorate markedly. Although during their stay in office the military officers had sought to introduce reforms that would remedy some of the worst abuses of higher education, they had, in fact, achieved little of consequence. Hoping to rejuvenate the universities, they had expelled 147 professors who were felt to be incompetent, though many were actually dismissed for personal or political reasons. The result was not that university problems were resolved, but that tensions increased, and even more conflicts were created as the outcry from the intellectuals and the students eventually led to the reinstatment of the dismissed faculty members whose positions had, in the meantime, been filled by other professors. Nor were the other reform measures—strengthening the autonomy of the universities, which thus became practically immune from outside control, and amending the chair system so as to provide more rights to junior faculty—much more successful. All these steps resulted in little fundamental change in administrative and academic procedures and, indeed, the high degree of autonomy served to further hinder efforts at change and innovation (Weiker, 1963: 48-63; Karayalçin, 1964; Forum, 1965; T.C. Senatosu, 1965).

Moreover, here, too, the story of the fifties was once again repeated as enrollments continued to grow inexorably and facilities became more strained than ever. Not only did this expansion take place with but limited relevance to the country's manpower needs, but the increases in physical and human resources did not match those in student enrollments, so that all the many problem areas which confronted Turkish universities in the fifties were significantly aggravated. Nor did the establishment of a national examination which screens out a high percentage of all students diminish pressures upon the universities, because political considerations proved irresistible and enrollments could not be limited to desired levels. The first five-year plan, for example, provided for an increase in enrollments from 63,000 in 1963 to 88,000 by 1967, but 126,000 students were enrolled in 1968. As a result, standards continued to decline, and, according to the second five-year plan, less than 20% of the students enrolled in the Law Faculty of Istanbul University since 1960 have graduated; of every 100 students registered in the Faculty of Letters, only 15 ever continue their studies, and a mere 6 graduate.

Moreover, pedanticism, scholasticism, rigidity, and formalism remain the norm. The goal is still to memorize the content of the lecture notes as exactly as possible in order to pass the examinations, and few teachers devote much time to students outside the classroom. The consequences of such an educational experience are, of course, profound, and one American scholar (Cohn, 1970: 110), well acquainted with the Turkish educational system, has argued that the students' ideological orientations are directly shaped by it:

> Graduates of Turkish schools are not discriminating in their approach to facts. They often accept without critical examination statements that are alleged to be true but are in fact wrong. They also seem to have more than ordinary difficulty in distinguishing fact from guess or mere hope and in sorting out the plausible from the implausible. . . . The tendency to seek simple black-or-white answers to complex questions, instead of recognizing that truth is frequently gray, seems to be another consequence of the oversimplified right-or-wrong approach followed in Turkish instruction.

> The present appeal of Marxism to Turkish youth, although partly due to youthful idealism and partly due to the circumstances that it was for a long time taboo and therefore seems especially daring, is also in part attributable to the fact that it claims to provide authoritative black-or-white answers to all the problems of society.

Such environmental conditions made for marked student frustration, and university reform became a national issue in the sixties. How deeply students feel about this question is indicated by the results of a national survey conducted in 1967 which asked students to rank the areas of most concern to them. Problems connected with the academic environment accounted for almost half of all answers. Physical inadequacies were dealt with by 26%, who complained of inadequate dormitory and canteen facilities and pointed specifically to limited numbers of showers, lack of space to study, poor comfort, and a general lack of discipline and organization within the dormitories. Another 21 percent focused upon academic issues and complained of the ways in which courses were conducted, the worries caused by the examinations, the difficulties of attending a faculty in which the student had little interest, and so forth (Baymur, 1969: 63). Further indication of the degree of student discontent with the university environment is provided by a study conducted at Istanbul Technical University in the late 1960s. Eighty-three % declared that they did not consider their education adequate and in answer to a question concerning major weaknesses, 64 percent listed the method of teaching; 42 percent were also dissatisfied with their living arrangements; 50 percent, with their meals (ITU, 1969). Another major area of student concern involves their economic position. Like the 1950s, the 1960s were marked by a high rate of inflation, and many students complained of inadequate income and at the same time expressed concern at the burden which they were imposing upon their families. Students were also worried about male-female relations, lack of social-cultural facilities, and general personal problems (Baymur, 1969: 62).

Under these conditions, it is not surprising that questions of university administration and reform came to represent a major focus of their activism. It is, however, important to note that important differences characterize the eight universities that now exist in Turkey, for, during these years, Turkish higher education became increasingly differentiated, and new universities with structures and processes that differed considerably from the traditional patterns were established and developed. At present, there are three such institutions within the country: Ataturk University in Erzerum, the Middle East Technical University, and Haceteppe University, both in Ankara. The other five—the University of Istanbul, Istanbul Technical University, Ankara University, the Aegean University in Izmir, and the Black Sea University in Trabzon—are structured along traditional lines.

This development, however, was not welcomed by all those concerned with higher education, and, in fact, a considerable amount of conflict soon became evident between representatives of the more traditional institutions who fought for a uniform system, and advocates of greater flexibility and differentiation of functions. What this means for Turkish higher education has been well described by a knowledgeable Turkish educator (Okyar, 1968: 221):

We are at present facing the difficult problems of coping with unprecedented numbers while trying to raise standards of teaching and research which the existing traditions and practices of the Turkish universities and of other higher educational institutions do not seem able to solve. The present university system, composed on one side of old-established universities, which are extremely large and cumbersome, attached to their own *status quo* and showing little capacity even to paper over their internal differences with agreed common proposals for change, and, on the other side, of new universities which have not all yet found their balance and sense of direction, has to be closely and critically examined.

Given the inability of the authorities to effect changes in higher education, it is not surprising that students soon began to attempt to actively involve themselves in the functioning of the universities. Beginning with the opposition by the student associations to the firing of the 147 professors, students both within and outside their organizations made frequent attacks upon the universities. They staged boycotts and demonstrations on a wide variety of academic issues and, in 1964, they even refused to attend the official ceremony marking the beginning of the school year at Istanbul University. They held their own ceremony in protest against conditions at the university, demanded immediate reforms, and publicly accused the faculty and administrators of various immoral and illegal acts (Yeni Gazete, 1964). These bitter charges, which stemmed from a government plan to increase fees, shattered whatever remained of the unity which had previously existed within the academic community and marked a new low in faculty-student relations.

Student frustration with academic matters reached a high point in 1968, when a series of boycotts, strikes, and demonstrations affected most faculties and higher institutes.[11] An incident in the Religious Faculty of Ankara University quickly sparked a boycott that spread to the agricultural faculties of Erzerum, Ankara, and Aegean universities. From there, boycotts soon affected other Ankara University faculties, and it was not long before Istanbul and Aegean University faculties also joined in.

In the course of these events, students openly articulated their intense dissatisfaction with the quality of their educational experience. They demanded educational reforms and a new law governing the universities. Specifically, they complained of overcrowded classes and the autocratic and impersonal attitudes of the faculty, and sought a more democratic and open relationship in and out of the classroom. A second major demand was for an end to the practice (by all universities except METU and Haceteppe) of employing part-time faculty. Although the law decreed that faculty members could spend only ten hours a week in other occupations, this law was frequently violated, and most professors devoted far more attention to their outside activities—practicing engineering, medicine, or law, and teaching in private schools—than to their faculty. They also demanded that the traditional practice of not permitting assistants with their Ph.D. to teach be changed. Other student demands included participation in the administration of faculties, additional rights in examinations, equality of opportunity for all students, and the nationalization of private schools which had proliferated in the sixties as the state universities proved incapable of meeting the demand for higher education. Critics—including practically all university students—claimed that quality was low, that they were employing faculty from the regular universities who thus devoted even less time to their regular duties, and that their graduates could not be absorbed by the economy (Tezcan, 1969).

The last point reflects the degree to which students in this period could be described as suffering from feelings of relative deprivation. Throughout these demonstrations, they raised many issues related both to their immediate socioeconomic environment (lower book prices, more credits and fellowships, improvements in dormitories and canteens) and to their future opportunities. Students in the agricultural and forestry faculties demanded changes in the conditions under which they could be hired by the government: the law, economics, and medical faculties of Istanbul University published a joint communique demanding positions after graduation; and students in science and literature faculties issued declarations demanding that they be made eligible for positions in lycées upon completing their education. In short, students in a wide range of disciplines were particularly concerned with their future opportunities.

In at least two respects, these 1968 demonstrations mark a watershed in the history of the Turkish student movement. First, the regular student unions were not really involved in what was essentially a spontaneous, nonideological uprising. As we have noted, their influence and power had dropped steadily during the decade, and, from now on their role was to be filled by new, militant, ideological associations. In these events, however, the influence of both left- and right-wing groups and faculty members was originally limited. The students declared their autonomy and were apparently concerned solely with educational reforms, but their unity was short-lived, as ideological considerations soon divided them. The students of the Political Science Faculty demonstrated in support of the boycotts with signs demanding an end to American imperialism, Turkish withdrawal from NATO, and the like. Rightist students promptly withdrew their support and moved to break the movement through various means, including attacks with dynamite.[12]

The use of such weapons marks the second reason why 1968 represents a turning point. From then on, violence became the norm, as the new groups that replaced the older associations proved far more militant and willing to utilize violence to achieve their goals. These groupings represented both the extreme right and the extreme left. The most important of the right-wing groups were the "Commandos" organized by the CKMP, a political party that espouses an ideology containing blends of national socialism, reformism, and authoritarianism. The Commandos received paramilitary training in special camps and, from 1968 onward, were involved in a large number of violent incidents. MTTB also had its share of violent reactionaries in its ranks, and, by the late sixties, the militants of the right were estimated at 300-400 persons (Genç, 1971: 295).

The most important of the leftist organizations was the FKF (Intellectual Club Federation) whose roots dated back to the early sixties when one club was formed in the Political Science Faculty of Ankara University. In the spring of 1965, some of its members and some youths who were TIP supporters were distributing a magazine published by TIP, when they were attacked in the center of Ankara. The result was to unite these two groups and new *Fikir Klubs* were formed and brought together into a federation (Toker, 1971: 53).

At first, FKF was controlled by TIP, but before long the dissensions within that party's elite were reflected within FKF. At least three factions were evident within TIP, and, when one—headed by Mihri Belli, who advocated a "popular front" strategy—was expelled, its supporters captured control of FKF in 1968. The struggle for power within FKF continued unabated, however, and subsequently TIP regained control of FKF (Genç, 1971: 96, 141).

In October 1969, FKF reorganized itself as *Dev Genç* (Revolutionary Youth Federation). The new organization soon spread rapidly in all faculties and higher institutes and gained control of the student associations therein. From these associations, Dev Genç secured an income reputedly of 3 million TL per year, which it used to further its own ends. Some of its members were also sent to the Palestinian guerrillas for training in the use of tactics and weaponry, and soon Dev Genç was reputed to have 600 trained militants. Dev Genç moved to extend its influence within the faculties by supporting various professors for office who were sympathetic for ideological or other reasons, and before long the organization was a power in many faculties (Genç, 1971: 293 ff., 122, 141).

Despite its strength, however, Dev Genç, like its predecessor, suffered from severe internal dissension. The consensus concerning the desirability of using violence to bring down the government did not extend to strategy; adherents of both urban guerrilla warfare and rural insurgency were to be found within its ranks and soon four distinct groups could be identified within the organization (Genç, 1971: 345; Toker, 1971: 92).

Thus the stage was set for a violent confrontation between the extreme left and the extreme right and for reliance upon guerrilla tactics by the militant leftists. The orientation of the two extremes toward violence is reflected in the following quotes by their spokesmen, who participated in a round table in 1970. The Dev Genç leader stated: "Youth is the dynamite cap and will continue to play this role until the social dynamite explodes. . . . There is no democracy in Turkey. . . . We must arm ourselves for self defense against reactionaries . . . unless the class struggle and the struggle against U.S. imperalism ends we cannot give up our weapons." The rightist spokesman replied: "This anarchy prevents people from understanding nationalism. . . . As long as the Marxist-Socialist groups directed by outside forces exist fighting will continue" (Genç, 1971: 4-11).

Fighting did continue, and a bloody toll of students was taken as one incident followed another. One particularly massive encounter occurred in February 1969 in conjunction with the scheduled visit of the U.S. Sixth Fleet to Istanbul—a favorite occasion for incidents—when a large demonstration, organized by radical students and trade unions, collided with right-wing elements. Several persons were killed and over 200 wounded, many seriously. Although this tragedy had a temporary, sobering effect, the approaching election made it inevitable that student political activism would remain at a high level, and other major incidents occurred in April when students at METU occupied the campus, denounced the government, and demanded academic reforms and political changes; in May, when the University of Istanbul was occupied by students and closed for several months; and in June, when riots involving students erupted in Istanbul and then in Ankara.

The 1969 elections did not diminish the tension within the country, for the AP was returned to power with a majority of the seats in parliament, but with only a minority of the popular vote. Furthermore, shortly thereafter, Mr. Demirel formed a cabinet without the representation of any members of the right wing of his party. A governmental crisis quickly ensued as 41 AP deputies voted against the budget. Though Mr. Demirel, after a one-month hiatus, was able to form a new government with the support of some minor parties and independents, the legitimacy of existing institutions was further strained, and violent confrontations between students wielding pistols, knives, clubs, dynamite, and gasoline bombs continued and even intensified. The government sought to repress this anarchy by closing several student associations in October 1969 on the grounds that they had engaged in political activities. In its efforts to restore order, the government was supported by İsmet İnönü, the head of the CHP, who denounced student extremism, as well as by the National Security Council. These measures did not reduce the level of violence; mutual kidnappings, reprisals, and accidental deaths continued unabated, as the precarious position of the regime further encouraged violence by militant groups. In February 1971, the government introduced stringent new legislation which provided prison terms for "interfering with commercial activity, occupying factories, making bombs, insulting or resisting officers . . . interfering with public services or road transport, and defacing official posters" (New York Times, 1971a). Nevertheless violence continued, and later that month over 220 students were arrested in Ankara following a battle with the police by Haceteppe University students who refused to permit a search of dormitories and hotels for weapons. The police action, an outgrowth of earlier disturbances, was opposed by students using pistols, Molotov cocktails, and dynamite. The extent to which popular feeling had turned against the students is evidenced by the fact that, during the shooting, student members of Dev-Genç were insulted and threatened by the crowd that gathered, and only police action prevented a student from being lynched by spectators (New York Times, 1971b).

Three weeks later, the military intervened. Feeling that the government was incapable of maintaining order, of restoring national unity, or of achieving the kind of development that was essential, the Turkish military leaders forced Prime Minister Demirel to resign. Since that time, energetic and repressive measures have been taken to halt student violence, and an era of unparalleled student activism has come to an end. Some students have continued to engage in acts of terrorism, but they represent an extremist, revolutionary fringe divorced from the student movement, which should be considered as a separate phenomenon.

The style, character, and intensity of the activism that occurred prior to the military intervention, does on the other hand, conform in many respects to our conceptual model. The political system was characterized

[66]

by low legitimacy in student eyes and by low repression, although late in the decade the government did seek to increase its level of control. Moreover, it was marked by a high degree of tension and competition between various political actors and groupings, many of whom were within the same party. The student subsystem was characterized by high degrees of frustration resulting from the steady deterioration of the academic environment and worsening future opportunities. International penetration in the form of alliances and ideologies deeply affected both the society as a whole and the students in particular. In addition, very close linkages existed between the student subsystem and the polity. We have emphasized the degree to which student factions were interacting with political groups and the consequences for the student movement that flowed therefrom. Our second linkage variable, relative deprivation, was also operative in this period, though it should be stressed that what might be termed "societal deprivation" was probably of far more importance to the extreme leftists than their perceptions of their own future opportunities. They were highly politicized and ideologically motivated and regarded the political system as illegitimate because in their view it could not meet the needs of oppressed social classes. Accordingly, they engaged in revolutionary activities and guerrilla warfare to destroy it. Their opponents on the right were motivated by similar considerations, though from an opposing ideological perspective, and were equally willing to utilize violence to prevent the emergence of a system that, in their eyes, would be as illegitimate as the present one was in the eyes of the leftists.

CONCLUSION

In this monograph, we have developed a model to permit the analysis of student activism longitudinally and comparatively, and we have applied it to the Ottoman Empire and the Turkish Republic in order to assess the degree to which it can serve to illuminate the dynamics of student activism in at least one particular instance. In general, it seems as though we have identified the major independent variables and that the model fits this particular case quite well. Nevertheless, it is also apparent that the complex of relationships among the variables we have discussed may, in fact, be more dynamically interdependent than was originally postulated.

Our first major variable set was the systemic context, within which we identified the political system as preeminent. We also suggested that international penetration would be of significance, and there seems to be a high correlation between the degree of penetration and the character and orientation of student activism. In each of the periods we have discussed, ideologies and events abroad had a profound impact upon students. In the Ottoman Empire, such values as nationalism, Westernization, and constitutionalism, all of which were imported from abroad, influenced student behavior, particularly in the military schools, and led to revolutionary activity directed against Sultan Abdul Hamid II. Even the religious students were affected by external pressures, though, in their case, the impact was not in terms of values but rather in terms of the consequences of the specific environmental changes that resulted in the nineteenth century when, beginning with Sultan Mahmud II, one sultan after another adopted a series of reform measures that transformed the character of Ottoman society, and, hence, of the religious institution. External forces were also to be an important variable in subsequent periods. After World War I, a nationalist reaction developed among the students and, during the Ataturk regime, the growth of Nazism, communism and fascism deeply affected Turkish society in general and the students in particular. Specific events that occurred abroad also led to reactions by students, the most obvious example being the Bulgarian cemetery incident and the question of Cyprus.

Implicit in this summary is the fact that subsumed within the concept "international penetration" are several separate and distinct phenomena, each of which affects student activism in different ways. The first of these involves general value and ideological trends that, originating outside the society, come to be known and more or less influential within it. We would place the growth of leftist ideologies in the sixties within this category. Here the result is to enhance fragmentation and conflict. A second dimension involves particular actions by foreign actors that provoke student reactions, as in the case of Cyprus. In such instances, the result is often unity manifested in a specific demonstration or series of demonstrations. Third, external events may influence the regime to adopt particular policies that lead to environmental change domestically, but the consequences for student activism will vary according to numerous societal and political variables.

It is for reasons such as this that we have argued that the political system must be considered the major independent variable that shapes student activism. Indeed, it has an impact upon all the components of the major variable set we have labelled the student subsystem, including the university environment, the structure of the student organizations, and the character of their membership and leadership. Quite clearly, political decisions determine the character and structure of higher education in any society, but it does not appear as though this dimension of the student subsystem represented a major independent variable over time. The quality of the educational experience or the physical facilities available to students does not seem to be directly related to activism. At most, one could suggest that this dimension represents an intervening variable and that under certain conditions students would demonstrate their frustrations with their immediate environment. This was particularly true in the late sixties when academic questions were a major target of activism but, even then, the factors making for activism and shaping its character lay outside the student subsystem itself and were to be found in the economic and political systems of the society.

The structure and functioning of the student organizations and the character of their leadership are particularly affected by the nature of the political system. The two political variables that we have focused upon are repression and legitimacy, and we have attempted to assess the degree to which they influence the character, intensity, and orientation of student structures and activities over time. Legitimacy does seem to represent a prime explanatory variable, particularly of the goals and targets of activism. In periods of low legitimacy—the empire of Abdul Hamid II, the later years of the Demirel and Menderes governments—student activism was broadly directed against all levels of the political system. In other periods, however—such as the Turkey of Ataturk or the first half of the fifties when the polity was characterized by high legitimacy—student activism was specifically directed, the goal of the students being not to bring about governmental change but, at most, a shift in a particular policy, and, in many cases, the targets of student activism were external actors.

Repression, on the other hand, shapes the character of student activism and the channels through which it is expressed. Under conditions of high repression, formal student organizations are either forbidden or tightly controlled and their activities carefully circumscribed. In these periods, student organizations are oriented toward local concerns, though they may also be mobilized to support the regime in various ways. Repression, however, interacts with legitimacy in many ways to determine the character of student activism. Should repression and legitimacy both be high, then the level of activism will be low, spontaneous, and short-lived or else sponsored by the government. Should legitimacy be low, then, as in the reign of Abdul Hamid II, activism will be secret, continuous, and revolutionary. Despite the repressiveness of that ruler, however, activism could not be destroyed, and ultimately the Sultan was overthrown by the Young Turks. This event highlights the limits of student activism—it can serve as the catalyst for revolution, but without allies able to exercise power, particularly the military, it cannot effect systemic change. Moreover, a sharp contrast exists between the efficacy of repression during periods of high and low legitimacy. Under Ataturk, decisions to put an end to student activism were quickly and effectively carried out, and it appears that the greater the legitimacy of the regime, the more effective will be increases in repression directed against student activism.

Events in the late fifties and sixties support this hypothesis and provide further insights into the importance of repression as a major independent variable. In this period of essentially low repression, students were active and influential political actors. They engaged in negotiations with university administrators and government officials and enjoyed close linkages with a variety of political actors. Indeed, the structure and character of the student movement in the past two decades reflected to a remarkable degree developments within the polity. The student organizations essentially mirrored the major groupings within the political system, and increases in fragmentation and political tensions resulted in a proliferation of formal or informal student groups and factions who were involved in numerous boycotts, demonstrations, and violent incidents of all sorts.

The leadership of the student organizations was also deeply affected by these developments, and the organizations passed into the hands of students who were quite willing to sacrifice their academic careers in order to achieve political success later. The emergence of such leaders had profound consequences for the organizations themselves and for their coherence and effectiveness. As leadership became a more and more valued political good, so did the tactics used to achieve control deteriorate, until unorthodox tactics and violence became commonplace. One result of this development was to severely damage the student organizations both in the eyes of the majority of the students and of the public in general, so that only a small minority of all students continued to be active or even interested in the traditional organizations or the newer, and even more politically oriented, ones that emerged.

This discussion of the relationship between political variables and the student subsystem has emphasized not only the importance of such dimensions as repression and legitimacy, but also indicates the dynamic interrelationship between variables referred to earlier. The character of the polity directly influences the linkage variables that we have identified, particularly the ties between students and political actors. Such ties existed in all periods but, depending upon the degree of legitimacy of the polity and of its repressive control, the character of these ties differed sharply. Essentially, it appears as though repression and linkages with political actors are negatively related; the less repressive the system, the more numerous, intense, and open the interaction. The effect of this interaction, however, depends upon such variables as the character and composition of political factions, their interrelationships, and the level of tension within the polity. Hence, the result of establishing various political party branches among the students (formally or informally) is fragmentation and polarization to a greater or lesser degree. Indeed, it would be no exaggeration to suggest that all political actors exploited students for their own advantage and that governments and opponents alike sought to activate or deactivate students in order to achieve particular political objectives.

Our second linkage variable, relative deprivation, seems to function as the essential prerequisite, a catalytic fuse that predisposes students toward active outbreaks of one sort or another. It is, however, important to note the extent to which the two forms of relative deprivation that we have identified have assumed salience at different times. The first aspect involves a concern for one's own future opportunities and, as we have seen, student activism often occurred in periods when prospects were not particularly bright for students. This was particularly true of the time of Abdul Hamid, the years of the world depression, and the late fifties. In recent years, however, a different aspect of relative deprivation has become particularly salient for many students, the perceived deprivation of other societal groups. In this case, students regard the allocation of social and economic goods as inequitable and believe that various social groups are denied a just share of the nation's output. The slogan "social justice," which became current in the sixties, reflects this concern.

The linkage with legitimacy also differs somewhat depending upon the type of relative deprivation involved. In most periods, dismal student perceptions of future opportunities coincided with low regime legitimacy. In some cases, however, notably in the twenties and thirties, regime and government legitimacy remained high even though there were many indications that students were subject to feelings of relative deprivation. Hence, one may suggest that, under conditions of dynamic charismatic leadership, feelings of relative deprivation must be considerably aggravated before even government legitimacy is affected. In such cases, relative deprivation will provoke student activism which will be directed against a specific policy or actor. When students possess feelings of "societal deprivation," however, then, almost by definition, the government and the "rules of the game" are both viewed as illegitimate, and the purpose of activism is to bring about systemic change through organized revolutionary violence.

International penetration is of particular importance in this regard, for it is clear that these radical students have been deeply influenced by ideological currents operant within the international system and that they share the values, tactics, and objectives of similar groups in other societies. Thus, the character of the domestic political system once again assumes major importance, for its characteristics will determine the degree of such penetration and the extent to which terrorist activities can be carried out. Essentially, the military has, since 1971, greatly increased the level of control and repression within the society and has ended all political activities by student associations. Martial law was proclaimed, and, though a few "guerrillas" organized in the Turkish Peoples Liberation Army appear able to carry out terrorist acts, the level of violence has declined markedly. Political development, however, has entered a new phase, and major political system characteristics remain to be definitely delineated. In terms of our model, the degree of legitimacy accorded to the polity will be one of the most important determinants of the future shape of student activism, and much therefore depends upon the quality of the new leadership and its effectiveness in responding to the many problems confronting Turkey today.

NOTES

1. For an introduction to the voluminous literature on students, see Emmerson (1968), Lipset (1967) and Altbach and Laufer (1971).

2. The published literature consists essentially of two articles, one by Roos et al. (1969) which focuses primarily upon political socialization and one by Szyliowicz (1970) that uses some of the data presented in this monograph to describe briefly the historical development of the student movement.

3. Davison (1963: 325-327) suggests that the demonstrations were at least partly spontaneous.

4. In 1914, the Law School had 2,119 students; theology and letters, 348; sciences, 200—for a total of 2,667. No data are available for the Medical School (Berkes, 1964: 378).

5. On the founding of the Türk Ocaklari see Taylak (1969: 68-78) and Tunaya (1952: 378 ff.); on Gökalp's influence among the youth, see Heyd (1950: 32-33, 36).

6. These events were reported in the Istanbul press. For details, see Vakit (1933) and Son Posta (1933); see also Taylak (1969: 125 ff.).

7. I was permitted to examine the unpublished records of these meetings, the MTTB "Karar Defteri." The quote is from the entry for the meeting of January 26, 1934.

8. According to another study, 65 percent of the students at Istanbul University had an income of 250 TL a month or less in the mid-sixties (Mediko-Sosyal Merkezi 1965: 11).

9. For a discussion of political developments in this period, see Dodd (1969), Sherwood (1967), Karpat (1967), Ulman and Tachau (1965), Szyliowicz (1966a), and Hyland (1970).

10. Some persons claimed that the signature was genuine, having been obtained by devious means, but that the letter itself was a forgery.

11. In the 1967-1968 academic year, failure rates were 56 percent for medicine, 59 percent for law, 50 percent for literature, 68 percent for dentistry, and 10 percent for forestry (Mediko-Sosyal Merkezi, 1968: 12).

12. For the claim that the boycotts were essentially nonpolitical, see Tezcan (1969: 173 ff.). Genç (1971: 117 ff.), on the other hand, traces their politicization.

REFERENCES

ABADAN, N. (1963) "Values and political behavior of Turkish youth," pp. 81-103 in Turkish Yearbook of International Relations. Ankara: Ankara Universitesi Basimevi.

——— (1961) Üniversite Öğrencilerinin Serbest Zaman Faaliyetleri. Ankara: Ankara Üniversitesi Basimevi.

ABADAN, Y. (1965) "Üniversitelerimiz ve sorunlari." Milliyet (January 11).

AKDAG, M. (1963) Celali Isyanlari. Ankara: Bilinmez Yayinevi.

ALTBACH, P. G. and R. S. LAUFER [eds.] (1971) "Students protest." Annals of Amer. Academy of Pol. and Social Sci. (May): 395.

ARIBURNU, K. (1951) Milli Mucadele de İstanbul Mitingleri. Ankara: Bilinmez Yayinevi.

BAŞGOZ, İ. and H. E. WILSON (1968) Educational Problems in Turkey 1920-1940. The Hague: Mouton.

BAYMUR, F. (1969) "Yurtlarda kalan yüksek öğrenim Gençlerinin başlica problemleri." Haceteppe Sosyal ve Beşeri Bilimler Dergisi (March): 57-71.

BERKES, N. (1964) The Development of Secularism in Turkey. Montreal: McGill Univ. Press.

BILSEL, C. (1943) İstanbul Üniversitesi Tarihi. Istanbul: İstanbul Üniversitesi Yayinlari.

BWY, D. P. (1971) "Political instability in Latin America: the cross-cultural test of a causal model," pp. 113-141 in J. Gillespie and B. Nesvold (eds.) Macro-Quantitative Analysis. Beverly Hills: Sage Pubns.

COHN, E. J. (1970) Turkish Economic, Social, and Political Change. New York: Praeger Special Studies in International Economics and Development.

DAVIES, J. C. (1969) "The J curve of rising and declining satisfaction as a cause of some great revolutions and a contained rebellion," pp. 671-709 in H. Graham and T. Gurr (eds.) The History of Violence in America. New York: Bantam.

DAVISON, R. (1963) Reform in the Ottoman Empire. Princeton: Princeton Univ. Press.

Devlet İstatistik Enstitusu (1967). Milli Eğitim Hareketleri, 1927-1966. Ankara.

Devrim Gençliği (1965) "Mr Hicterin Raporu." July.

DODD, C. H. (1969) Politics and Government in Turkey. Manchester, Eng.: Manchester Univ. Press.

EASTON, D. (1965) A System Analysis of Political Life. New York: John Wiley.

EDIP, H. (1926) Memoirs. London: John Murray.

EMIN, A. (1914) The Development of Modern Turkey as Measured by Its Press. New York: Columbia Univ. Press.

EMMERSON, D. K. [ed.] (1968) Students and Politics in Developing Nations. New York: Frederick A. Praeger.

ERGIN, O. (1941) Maarif Tarihi. Istanbul: Osmanbey Matbaasi.

FEIERABEND, I. K., R. L. FEIERABEND, and B. A. NESVOLD (1969) "Social change and political violence: cross-national patterns," pp. 606-668 in H. Graham and T. Gurr (eds.) The History of Violence in America. New York: Bantam.

Forum (1965) "Üniversite meselesi." March 1 and March 15.

GENÇ, S. (1971) 12 Martá Nasil Gelindi. Ankara: İleri Yayinlari.

Gençlik (1965) "Gençlik kuruluşlarinda reform niçin gereklidir." (February): 10-11.

GÖHALP, A. (1961) "Turkish democracy betrayed." Phoenix (Queens's College; November 28).

GOLDRICH, D. (1966) Sons of the Establishment: Elite Youth in Panama and Costa Rica. Chicago: Rand McNally.

GURR, T. R. (1970) Why Men Rebel. Princeton: Princeton Univ. Press.

——— (1969) "A comparative study of civil strife," pp. 544-596 in H. Graham and T. Gurr (eds.) The History of Violence in America. New York: Bantam.

HERSHLAG, Z. Y. (1960) Turkey: An Economy in Transition. The Hague: Van Keulen.

HEYD, U. (1950) Foundations of Turkish Nationalism. London: Luzac-Harvill.

HORN, J. L. and P. KNOTT (1971) "Activist youth of the 1960's: summary and progress." Science 171 (March 12): 977-985.

HYLAND, M. P. (1970) "Crisis at the polls: Turkey's 1969 elections." Middle East J. 24 (Winter): 1-16.

İnkilap Gençliği (1952) September 23.

İPEKCI, A. and O. S. COŞAR (1965) İhtilâlin İçyüzü. İstanbul: Uygun Yayinevi.

İTÜ (1969) Oğrencilerinin Sosyal Durum Anketi Sonuçlari. İstanbul: İstanbul Teknik Üniversitesi İnşaat Fakültesi Matbaasi.

İÜTB (n.d.) "İstanbul Üniversitesi Talebe Birliği Olaganustu Kongre Gerekcesi." (mimeo)

KARAYALCIN, Y. (1964) Üniversitelerin İdare ve Murakabesi. Ankara: Ajans-Türk Matbaasi.

KARPAT, K. H. (1967) "Socialism and the Labor Party of Turkey." Middle East J. 21 (Spring): 157-172.

——— (1959) Turkey's Politics. Princeton: Princeton Univ. Press.

KAZAMIAS, A. (1966) Education and the Quest for Modernity in Turkey. Chicago: Univ. of Chicago Press.

KEMAL, G. M. (1929) A Speech. Leipzig: K. F. Koehler.

KENNISTON, K. (1965) The Uncommitted. New York: Harcourt, Brace & World.

——— and M. LERNER (1970) "The unholy alliance against the campus." New York Times Magazine (November 8).

KLINEBERG, S. (1971) "Modernization and the adolescent experience: a study of Tunisia." Key Reporter 37 (Autumn): 2-4.

KOPLIN, R. (1968) "A model of student politicization in the developing nations." Comparative Pol. Studies I (October): 373-390.

LEWIS, B. (1961) The Emergence of Modern Turkey. London: Oxford Univ. Press.

LIPSET, S. M. (1970) "American student activism in comparative persepective." Amer. Psych. 25 (August): 675-693.

——— (1968a) "The possible effects of student activism on international politics," pp. 495-521 in S. Lipset and P. Altbach (eds.) Students in Revolt. Boston: Houghton Mifflin.

——— (1968b) "The activists: a profile." Public Interest 13 (Fall): 39-51.

——— [ed.] (1967) Student Politics. New York: Basic Books.

London Times (1960) April 30.

MTTB (1953) "Çalişma raporu." (mimeo)

——— (n.d.) "Karar defteri." (unpublished)

MARDIN, S. (1962) The Genesis of Young Ottoman Thought. Princeton: Princeton Univ. Press.

MEARS, E. G. (1924) Modern Turkey. New York: Macmillan.

Mediko-Sosyal Merkezinin (1968) "1967 Yili Calişma raporu ile 1968—Yili Calişma raporu." Istanbul.

——— (1965) "1964 Yili Calişma raporu." Istanbul.

MIHÇIOĞLU, C. (1962) Üniversiteye Giriş Sinavlarinin Yeniden Düzenlenmesi. Ankara: Türkiye ve Orta Doğu Amme İdaresi Enstitusu.

New York Times (1971a) February 11.

——— (1971b) February 21.

OKYAR, O. (1968) "Universities in Turkey." Minerva 6 (Winter): 213-243.

ORGA, I. (1958) Phoenix Ascendant. London: Robert Hale.

Organization for Economic Cooperation and Development (1965) Turkey. Paris.

OZANKAYA, O. (1966) Universite Oğrencilerinin Siyasal Yönelimleri. Ankara: Ankara Universitesi Yayinlari.

PINNER, F. A. (1971) "Students—a marginal elite in politics." Annals of Academy of Pol. and Social Sci. 305 (May): 127-138.

RAMSAUR, E. E., Jr. (1957) The Young Turks. Princeton: Princeton Univ. Press.

REDDEN, K. (1957) Legal Education in Turkey. Istanbul: İstanbul Üniversitesi Hukuk Fakultesi Yayinlari.

ROOS, L. L., Jr., N. ROOS, and G. FIELD (1969) "Students and politics in Turkey," pp. 257-282 in S. Lipset and P. Altbach (eds.) Students in Revolt. Boston: Houghton Mifflin.

SARÇ, O. C. (1966) "Higher education in Turkey" pp. 101-110 in Education as a Factor of Accelerated Economic Development. Istanbul: Economic and Social Studies Conference Board.

SCOTT, J. W. and M. El-ASSAL (1969) "Multiversity, university quality and student protest: an empirical study." Amer. Soc. Rev. 34 (October): 702-709.

Son Posta (1933) February 26-March 1: April 21-28.

SHERWOOD, W. B. (1967) "The rise of the Justice Party in Turkey." World Politics 20 (October): 54-65.

SZYLIOWICZ, J. S. (1970) "Students and politics in Turkey." Middle Eastern Studies 6 (May): 150-162.

——— (1966a) "The Turkish elections: 1965." Middle East J. 20 (Autumn): 473-494.

——— (1966b) "Political participation and modernization in Turkey." Western Pol. Q. 19 (June): 266-284.

TAYLAK, M. (1969) Öğrenci Hareketleri. Ankara: Basnur Matbaasi.

T. C. Senatosu (1965) "Universitelerimizin verimini artirmak, sīkīntīlara çare bulmak için neler yapilabileceğinin tâyin ve tesbiti maksadiyle kurulmuş bulunan Araştirma Komisyonu Raporu." Araştirma Komisyounu Başkanliği Sayī 10/4.

TMTF (1963) "XVII devre genel baskanlīk çalisma ve muhasebe raporu." (mimeo)

——— (1954) "9 devre faaliyet raporu: 5 Nisan 1953-22 Mart 1954." (mimeo)

——— (n.d.) "Report on Turkey in the Student Welfare Conference of Istanbul." (mimeo)

TEZCAN, M. (1969) "Memleketimizin yüksek ögrenim kurumlarinda ögrenci hareketleri ve ortaya çikardigi sorunlar," pp. 167-205 in 1968 Yili Ögrenci Hareketleri (Dunyada ve Türkiye' de). Ankara: Ankara Üniversitiesi Eğitim Fakültesi Yayīnlari 7.

TOKER, M. (1971) Solda ve Sağda Vuruşanlar. Ankara: Akis Yayīnlari.

TOYNBEE, A. J. and K. KIRKWOOD (1927) Turkey. New York: Charles Schribner.

TUNAYA, T. Z. (1952) Türkiyede Siyasi Partiler. Istanbul: Doğan Kardeş Yayīnlari A. Ş. Basimevi.

Turkey, Republic of (1969) Second Five Year Development Plan 1968-1972. Ankara: State Planning Organization.

——— (1963) First Five Year Development Plan 1963-1967. Ankara: State Planning Organization.

TYGART, C. E. and N. HOLT (1972) "Examining the Weinberg and Walker typology of student activists." Amer. J. of Sociology 77 (March): 957-966.

ULMAN, A. H. and F. TACHAU (1965) "Turkish politics: the attempt to reconcile rapid modernization with democracy." Middle East J. 19 (Spring): 153-168.

Vakit (1933) February 26-March 1; April 21-28.

WEIKER, W. (1963) The Turkish Revolution (1960-1961). Washington, D.C.: Brookings Institution.

WEINBERG, I. and WALKER, K. N. (1969) "Student politics and political systems: toward a typology." Amer. J. of Sociology 75 (July): 77-96.

YAZICI, T. (1966) "Softa." Islam Ansiklopedisi 9: 735-736.

Yeni Gazete (1964) November 2.

Yeni İstanbul (1965) March 21.

Yeni Milli Birlik (1949) December 15.

Yeni Sabah (1953) January 16.

APPENDIX
FATHERS' OCCUPATIONS (in percentages)

	(1) Ankara University (1961)	(2) Ankara University (1961)	(3) Ankara University (1962)	(4) Ankara University (1966)	(5) Istanbul University (1965)	(6) All Universities (1962)	(7) Istanbul University (1967)	(8) Istanbul Tech. Univ. (1969)
Bureaucrats	34	39	41	54	21	37	19	23
Army Officers	–	6	–	–	8	4	12	6
Professionals	8	14	–	6	18	–	20	18
Businessmen, Merchants	16	19	23	16	20	33	25	26
Farmers	19	13	15	16	16	17	8	17
Workers	6	4	–	6	18	8	6	11
Others	18	5	26	3	–	–	10	–

SOURCE: The figures are derived from the following:

Column 1—Mihçioğlu (1962: 58)
Column 2—Abadan (1961: 18)
Column 3—TMTF (1963: 6; the original does not add up to 100%)
Column 4—Ozankaya (1966: 21)
Column 5—Mediko-Sosyal Merkezi (1965:12)
Column 6—TMTF (1963: 6)
Column 7—Mediko-Sosyal Merkezi (1968: 10)
Column 8—ITÜ (1969: 2)

JOSEPH S. SZYLIOWICZ is Associate Professor in the Graduate School of International Studies at the University of Denver, where he has been affiliated since 1965, and where he also serves as Editor of the Monograph Series in World Affairs. He previously taught with Long Island University, Brooklyn and Hunter colleges, and the University of Maryland. He has authored many articles on Turkey, and his books include The Contemporary Middle East, Tradition and Innovation *(coedited with Benjamin Rivlin),* Political Change in Rural Turkey, Erdemli: A Case Study, *and the forthcoming* Education and Modernization in the Middle East.